# A
# Book
# Of
# Christmas

# Readings for Reflection during Advent and Christmas

THE UPPER ROOM
*Nashville, Tennessee*

# A BOOK OF CHRISTMAS

While we have made every effort to contact all authors represented in this collection, in a few cases we were unable to do so. Please contact the publisher at the above address if you are one of those persons.

"Unwrapping the Crèche" and "A Place for Love" also appear in *On Time for Christmas,* copyright 1988 by Thomas John Carlisle.

"The Singing of Angels" and "The Work of Christmas" are from *The Mood of Christmas* © 1973 by Howard Thurman. Published 1973 by Harper & Row. Paperback edition published 1985 by Friends United Press, Richmond, Indiana.

Scripture quotations not otherwise identified or designated RSV are from the Revised Standard Version of the Bible, copyrighted 1946, 1952, and © 1971 by the Division of Christian Education, National Council of the Churches of Christ in the United States, and are used by permission.

Scripture quotations designated TEV are from the *Good News Bible, The Bible in Today's English Version,* copyright by American Bible Society, 1966, 1971, © 1976, and are used by permission.

Scription quotations designated NEB are from *The New English Bible,* © The Delegates of the Oxford University Press and the Syndics of the Cambridge University Press 1961 and 1970 and are used by permission.

Scripture quotations designated NIV are from the *Holy Bible: New International Version.* Copyright © 1973, 1978, 1984 International Bible Society. Used by permission of Zondervan Bible Publishers.

Scripture quotations designated PHILLIPS are from *The New Testament in Modern English,* by J. B. Phillips, and are used by permission of the Macmillan Company Copyright © 1958 by J. B. Phillips.

Scripture quotations designated JB are from *The Jerusalem Bible,* copyright © 1966 by Darton, Longman and Todd, Ltd. and Doubleday and Company, Inc. Used by permission of the publisher.

Scripture quotations designated NASB are from the *New American Standard Bible,* © The Lockman Foundation 1960, 1962, 1963, 1968, 1971.

Scripture quotations designated KJV are from the King James Version of the Bible.

Cover and Book Design: Jim Bateman
First Printing: September, 1988(10)
Library of Congress Catalog Card Number: 88-050244
ISBN 0-8358-0584-0

Printed in the United States of America

# Contents

# Preface

A *Book of Christmas* was born out of abundance. Since 1935 the publishing ministry of The Upper Room has flourished. Over the years, we have published many original meditations, articles, poems, prayers, and books which focus on themes especially appropriate for Advent and Christmas reflection. In this collection, we offer for the first time a sampling of some of the most thoughtful writings we have published in the last several years.

Each selection is identified by writer and by the magazine or book in which it first appeared. Our publishing ministry began with, and is still centered in, *The Upper Room* magazine. A biblically-based daily devotional guide, it is a channel for Christians to share their faith experiences and insights with other Christians around the world. Offering a unique approach to devotional life, *alive now!* is a bimonthly devotional magazine which explores one or more themes in each issue through photography, poetry, litanies, and brief meditative prose. *Pockets,* a colorful and carefully written monthly children's magazine, encourages six-to-twelve year olds in their faith development. *Weavings* is a bimonthly journal of the Christian spiritual life, offering articles, stories, poetry, practical guidance and book reviews by well-known writers. Upper Room Books publishes devotional resources for individuals and groups which encourage a disciplined approach to spiritual growth and which help people move toward spiritual maturity.

The goal of all Upper Room publishing is to encourage and guide people into a vital, intimate, and transforming relationship with God and help them to be connected to the larger Christian community of faith.

Christmas is a time of serious reflection and a time of great celebration. We hope the images and insights collected here will contribute to both your reflection and your celebration— this year and in years to come.

—Janice T. Grana
*World Editor and Publisher*

# Prologue

The four Sundays which precede Christmas Day itself are the calendar by which we mark the passing of the Advent season and the approach of the Christmas one. These have traditionally been times of retreat and introspection for Christians—if no longer to think penitentially on our sins, at least to consider with godly fear and joy the blending of our life into divine process.

In the church's scheme of things, Christmas as such begins, and Advent ends, with the birth of Our Lord. The Feast of the Nativity is usually celebrated by most Christians, of course, on Christmas Eve at the midnight service. But regardless of whether we date it on the twenty-fourth of December or the twenty-fifth, its joy becomes increasingly private over the course of our years, individualized into each heart so completely as to be almost universal and beyond the need of the telling.

The twelve days of Christmas come to an end on January 6, and the season of the Epiphany begins. But Epiphany not only ends Christmas; it also fulfills it by celebrating the revelation of the Christ to the whole world. The coming of Incarnate God to all people, especially to those of us who are Gentiles, is the bridge from birth into life, the event that makes Easter possible for most of us. The light of the Epiphany illuminates the church's year as it illuminates the human races from whom the kings came.

Holy seasons, like holy days, were not so much invented by the church as they were invented by life itself, I think. By common consent we hold to and preserve that which living has shown us contains the truths of both humankind and God.

I am not a cleric. I have never wanted to study in a

seminary or even to have access to one. I am instead a layperson, a writer and editor by trade, a woman. Over my fifty-odd years of living in cities and villages, mill towns and on farms, I have come increasingly to think that every believer must be a kind of psalmist, either literally or privately. That living itself has been given, at least in part, as a way of knowing God intimately. Every event takes on significance in that context, for there is no waste in experience. Every man and woman we meet becomes a metaphor of ourselves; every event, a simile, every thing, a symbol.

As Christians we are taught that our collective understanding and knowledge over the centuries since the coming of God have become, and are contained in, the liturgy and ritual of the church herself, the body of Christ passing itself on to each new member—part in the spiritual codes of symbol and sacrament, ritual and saint. Increasingly I find hope of the shared symbol's becoming once more the common language by which we rear our young and the mother tongue by which we all will someday cut the lines that separate us from one another...

We live in a culture still too new to yet have defined itself and under a government so young that my own lifetime has spanned a quarter of its history. In such times and circumstances I have found, in the heritage of the church, a transcendant purpose and connectedness for my own part of creation. For that I have always been grateful, both at Christmas and throughout the years.

—Phyllis A. Tickle
*What the Heart Already Knows*

# *One*

## Waiting

*I keep watch for the Lord,
I wait in hope for God our Saviour,
my God will hear me.*

Micah 7:7, TEV

# Unwrapping the Crèche

After the baby,
Joseph came next—
the adoring
guardian
of mother and child.
He watches me
as I tenderly
unwrap
the shepherds
and wise men
and a couple
of lullabying lambs.
Be careful,
he says,
the camels
can take care
of themselves,
but gently gather
my young
and beautiful
wife.
Remove the
swaddling wrappings
ever so lovingly
and place her
beside the manger,
for she
belongs with Jesus,
for she belongs to Jesus,
and I also,
I also.

—Thomas John Carlisle
   *Pockets*

# Waiting

Read Hosea 12:2–6

Hold fast to love and justice, and wait continually for your God.                                    —Hosea 12:6 (RSV)

Advent, like Lent, reminds us that there is value in waiting. Advent is our time to wait seriously for God to lead us from our self-imposed prisons such as our failures at love, our misunderstandings with others, our rigid belief-systems. Because such are our sins, we wait in bondage. Because we still want our way even if it is destructive, we pay a high price. We continue to follow after false gods of gadgetry or accumulations of possessions, power, and prestige. Meanwhile, the truly needy are truly neglected and the destitute truly ignored. No matter how we try to gloss it over, God will never accept our rationalizations.

And so this Advent we wait. We wait for a Savior. We wait for someone who can help us cut through all our false values and false pride. We wait for someone who not only knows our weaknesses but who, through the strength of a loving God, can help us overcome them. We wait for the one who forgives our failures and inspires us to try again.

Christ is coming. And his coming makes our waiting creatively and powerfully worthwhile.

*PRAYER:* We wait, O Lord, for the coming of your Word to us. May we not fail to hear and to see. Amen.

THOUGHT FOR THE DAY

When we wait for God, we never wait in vain.

—Stan Smith (North Carolina)
*The Upper Room*

# To Have a Vision

Read Isaiah 2:1–5

Where there is no vision, the people perish.
—Proverbs 29:18 (KJV)

A grapevine wreath hangs on our door year round. It keeps before us Isaiah's vision—a vision born at Christmas and made real by the Resurrection. During Advent, blue ribbon and white doves symbolizing Isaiah's peace with justice adorn the wreath. At Christmas, the white ribbon and a candle symbolize the Light born into the world. On Epiphany, January 6, red ribbon and stars mark the beginning of our journey to carry the Christmas vision, to follow a star. At Lent we remove everything but a purple ribbon, for Lent is a somber time to look inside ourselves. But at Easter, symbols of new life and opportunity to carry forth the vision—white ribbon, greens and butterflies—adorn our wreath.

At Pentecost, red ribbon and a descending white dove remind us that the Holy Spirit empowers us to carry the vision into an often hostile world. During Ordinary Time, green wraps the wreath, and we look for symbols to remind us that it is often in "ordinary times" that we have the opportunity all year to live out God's vision of peace and justice and love.

*PRAYER:* God, help us this Advent to see the vision you have given us. Amen.

THOUGHT FOR THE DAY

The Christmas vision means hope for tomorrow.

—Janet McNish Bugg (Tennessee)
*The Upper Room*

# All Because of That Baby

## A Children's Story

Jackson flipped the switch on the train and sent it spinning along the track. His eyes sparkled as it wove its way in and out among the few wrapped presents under the tree. Just as the train chugged through the tunnel, his mother called.

"Jackson!"

She sounded tired, the way she always did lately. "Honey, bring those clothes on up from the dryer. I need you to help fold."

Jackson made a face. Why did that baby have to be coming now, with Christmas almost here? He pushed the train lever impatiently, and his hand brushed the tiny wooden manger. His father had carved this set ten years ago, the Christmas after Jackson was born. Mama loved it, and she always insisted that it be under the tree, right in the very front.

Jackson stood up and trudged into the laundry room. Cora and Colby, the six-year-old twins, bounced a ball back and forth in the hallway. Jackson struggled to keep his balance as he squeezed by with the armload of clothes. "How about you two setting the table for dinner? Mama could use some more help, besides me." He tried to keep the bitterness out of his voice. It was no fun spending his whole Christmas vacation helping out at home, just because his mother was going to have a baby.

He floundered up the stairs, dropping several socks on the way. He stood for a moment by the front window. The wind sure was blowing. He was surprised at all the snow that had fallen in just this last hour. Jackson took the pile of clothes into the bedroom and dumped them on his mother's bed. She looked weary, but she smiled that special smile of hers. Jackson felt ashamed to be so grumpy, with Mama being so nice. He knew she didn't feel that great.

"This baby's getting might heavy, Jackson. The doctor said it might make its arrival in the next day or two."

Jackson folded towels with a vengeance, keeping his head down so Mama couldn't see the frown on his face. Tonight was Christmas Eve. Why couldn't that baby wait a few more days?

His mother sang softly along with the radio, "O Holy Night, the stars are brightly shining... it is the night of the dear savior's birth..." He had to admit she had a pretty voice.

"Mama, why did you and Daddy plan to have a baby this time of year? Wouldn't it be better to wait till the summer, when everything is all warm and nice?"

His mother looked at him, a smile playing around her lips. "Why, Jackson, this is a wonderful time of year to have a baby. Now, when everything is cold and dark, a baby will be a light and joy to us." Her eyes looked dreamy. "That's how I imagine the Christ Child himself, lighting up the cold and dark of all those lonely lives."

Mama talked that way sometimes. Jackson sighed. "We're not lonely. I like it just the way it is, with you and Daddy and me, and Cora and Colby."

His mother put down the towel she was folding. "Honey, there's always enough love to go around; now don't you forget it. Come here and give me a hug." She pulled Jackson toward her and laid a big smacking kiss on his cheek. Jackson made a face and pretended to pull away, but deep inside he liked it when she hugged him—even though he would never let her do it in front of the other boys.

The other boys were having a good time sledding on Clyde Hill. And here he was folding clothes—all because of that baby.

Mama winced and leaned on the pillow for a moment. "Be a sweetie, Jackson, and take the rest of those clothes into the other room to fold. I think I'll take a little rest."

Jackson looked at her anxiously. "Should I call Daddy and tell him to come on home from work early?"

Her voice sounded drowsy. "Guess it wouldn't hurt for you to give your daddy a call. Don't scare him, though. Most likely this baby will arrive sometime tomorrow morning."

Jackson gathered up the rest of the clothes and dumped

them on his own bed in the next room. Cora and Colby were making a terrific racket downstairs. It sounded as if they were throwing the ball against the ceiling. He went down and scolded them and turned on the afternoon cartoons.

He stood by the tree for a moment and looked longingly at the train. Here he was, having to babysit again. Couldn't even have time to play with his train set.

Jackson thought he heard Mama call, but he wasn't sure because the wind outside was getting so loud. This was some storm. He hoped Daddy would be able to get home tonight. He took the stairs two at a time and peered into the bedroom. "Did you call, Mama?"

She opened her eyes and gave him a weak smile. "This baby's just letting me know that he's getting ready to join us. Guess he's excited about Christmas, too. Have you called your daddy yet, honey?"

Jackson noticed how tightly his mother's hands were clenched. It worried him. "I'll call right now, Mama."

He picked up the phone in the living room, started to dial, then stopped. Something was wrong. There was no dial tone. He listened, shook the phone, then listened again. Still nothing.

Jackson grabbed his jacket and ran out the front door. Mrs. Wilson was right next door. He could use her phone.

He was surprised at the strength of the wind. It caught at him as soon as he stepped outside and spun him back against the door. He grabbed hold of the railing, hunched down low, and make his way down the few steps and across the little stretch of yard between the two houses. He slipped on Mrs. Wilson's icy porch and nearly fell, but caught hold of the doorknob.

She answered his knock almost immediately, a big smile lighting her face. "Why, Jackson, come on in. What are you doing out in this storm?"

Jackson tried to smile back at her, but his face felt numb already from the cold. "Could I use your phone, Mrs. Wilson? Ours isn't working."

"Oh, Jackson, I'm sorry. Mine isn't working either. I think the wind must have toppled one of the main wires. Is something wrong?"

Jackson took a deep breath. His knees felt a little weak, and a tiny anxious feeling began to form in the pit of his stomach. "It's Mama. She's going to have the baby pretty soon."

Mrs. Wilson looked worried. "Are you sure? Where's your daddy?"

Jackson felt like he was going to cry. "I was just going to call him at work. Now I can't call him. I can't call anybody to take mama to the hospital. Mama says not until tomorrow morning probably, but do you think it could be sooner?"

Mrs. Wilson's face relaxed. She pulled a pair of boots out from under the table. "I'm sure your mama knows better than either one of us. But I'll come back over with you and see if I can help. I've birthed many a baby; and, if need be, I'll help birth this one." Mrs. Wilson pulled on the boots and took her heavy coat from a hook on the kitchen door.

Jackson's stomach felt okay again. He pulled his jacket up around his ears, and the two of them struggled the short distance back in the howling wind.

Just as they came in the front door, Jackson heard a sudden sharp sound from the bedroom. Knees shaking, he hurried in. His mother had her eyes closed and was breathing rapidly. After a moment she opened her eyes and looked at Mrs. Wilson questioningly. Jackson explained, "Mama, the phones aren't working. But Mrs. Wilson says she'll stay."

Mrs. Wilson smiled her big warm smile. "I haven't birthed a baby for nearly two years now, so this will be a joy to me."

Jackson didn't feel scared now that Mrs. Wilson was here, but he felt mad. That baby! Coming on Christmas Eve, and ruining everything, all that special singing around the tree, and the big Christmas dinner. He felt great, angry words pressing against his throat; but he didn't want to say them, not when Mama was having the baby.

There was a great crash downstairs. Jackson jumped. He swallowed the angry words back down. "It's okay, Mama. Those crazy twins are just excited about Christmas. I'll go cool them down."

The twins stood by the Christmas tree looking guilty. The ball was behind the tree, its path traced by the two bare branches and a row of shattered ornaments on the floor. Jackson sighed. "Come on, you two. Let's clean up this mess. And be good now. Mama's having the baby."

Colby jumped up and started for the stairs. "She is? I want to go see."

Jackson caught his hand. "Not just yet, Colby. Mama needs quiet. Mrs. Wilson's with her, and I'm going to stay here with you. We'll go up later."

They had to move the presents to clean up the broken glass. Cora moved the nativity set, gently holding the little wooden baby in her hand. "See how sweet his face is, Jackson. How ever did Daddy do that, I wonder? I do love babies."

Jackson grunted. "They're a lot of trouble, if you ask me. Always coming at the wrong time, and causing all sorts of fuss when they do."

Cora stroked the little figure in her hand. "Was Baby Jesus a lot of trouble, do you think? Did he come at the wrong time?"

Jackson looked at her impatiently. "Of course not, silly. That was different. He..."

But Cora went on earnestly. "He came when Mary and Joseph were on a trip. They weren't even in their own house. And it was cold, and there wasn't room in the inn. My teacher said so. And he was born in a little stable, and there wasn't even a real crib to put him in. Only a wooden manger that the animals eat out of.

"Well, at least Mama has a real crib to put our baby in. And she has blankets, and Mrs. Wilson to help her," Colby said.

Jackson sat down in the rocker and pulled Cora onto his lap. Colby climbed up, too; and the three of them were quiet for a minute. Jackson gently took the little wooden figure from Cora's hand and looked at it. "I never thought of it that way before, Cora. I guess lots of people would say that Jesus came at the wrong time, like you said. Makes me think about what Mama told me. That he came at the right time to light up the cold and dark of all those lonely lives."

Cora's eyes shone. "Our baby will do that. Whenever I'm

lonely, when me and Colby have a fight, then I can go and hold our baby's hand, and I won't be lonely anymore. I think this is a good time to have a baby."

Jackson hugged the twins. "Maybe you're right, Cora."

—**Peggy King Anderson**
*Pockets*

# Waiting

As a child, I remember that the most difficult part of Christmas was simply waiting for it to arrive. From Thanksgiving to December 25 seemed more like an eternity than a month. Days seemed like weeks. Weeks felt like seasons. Time seemed to stand still.

Waiting is foreign to those of us who are accustomed to moving in the fast lane. Waiting seems unnatural. Knowing how to wait is, at best, an uncommon trait. We hunger for immediate satisfaction. The idea of delayed gratification is a stranger to our thinking.

Our society is alive with the symbols of our unwillingness or inability to wait. Exquisite taste does not sell TV dinners. Not having to prepare a meat-and-two-vegetable dinner is what makes this fare popular. Prepackaged vegetables in sealed bags are popular because they can easily be dropped in a 1½-quart pan of boiling water. Fast-food chains are booming because we can move through a little, crooked line, call out an order, sit down, eat, and rush on to the next lap of the rat race.

Condensed books are popular with busy people who do not have the patience to work through interesting sentence structure, innuendo, and the implications and subtleties of a great work. Time must be saved for greater responsibilities!

Many kitchens house Mr. Coffee machines; one simply spoons in the coffee and pours in water. The coffee is made before a cup can be found. In making the coffee this way, however, we miss the full "brew" of it. The rich aroma of the coffee does not drift through the house and into our nostrils as it did when it was perked or steeped. We give up the brew and the aroma in order to have it quickly.

People no longer want to dine. The leisurely meal, good conversation, and soft music are sacrificed for fast service, the check, the tip—and all because of busy schedules.

I can accept much of our no-wait approach to modern life, but I cannot bear instant potatoes. I like my potatoes baked until I can dress the soft white substance with hunks of butter and golf-ball-sized scoops of sour cream. I like to stir in the fixings until the steaming spud is ready to complement the entire meal. Instant potatoes cannot match that.

Waiting is difficult for modern people. We become ill, and we want to be made well now and not later. Medications, physicians, pastoral care, and love are often rejected if they are not swift. We want a miracle drug, the right prescription, and the best surgeon so that we can suddenly be back to our hurried routines. Six weeks out of seventy-five years is a low percentage of sick time to healthy time, but we must recover immediately because we do not know how to wait.

Though we do not like to wait, waiting is part of living. For example, we wait for peace. I might someday wait for my son-in-law to come home from Lebanon or Nicaragua. My mother waited for her brother to come home from World War II. My great-grandmother waited for her son to come home from World War I. Our forefathers and mothers have waited for tired, tattered soldiers to come home from Cuba, the Spanish War, the Civil War, the War of 1812, and the American Revolution.

For centuries believers and nonbelievers have had to live while waiting for something: peace, daylight, the recovery of sanity, or the coming of food stamps. Standing in line is commonplace. We have waited for a pass, a friend, a break, a payday, quitting time, death, the installments to be paid out, the family physician to come, prosperity, independence, comfort, the restoration of health, power, the Republicans to get in so the Democrats can get out, stocks to rise and fall, and the mailman. Waiting is not an option. It is part of living.

At the hospital, we pace in front of a swinging door marked "surgery." We wait for what is not yet, but for what is to be (or not to be). Living and waiting go hand in hand.

A colleague of mine recently learned that she was pregnant. Two days later she had signs of aborting the tiny fetus. Her physician assigned her to bed for twenty-four hours and said, "Wait." She said, "All I can do is wait. I feel helpless, as if the jury is out."

Waiting is like living in the meantime. It is like knowing

27

but not knowing. It is *how* one waits that matters.

God's clock is wound a different way. Time is different. Waiting, not hurrying, is one of God's characteristics. This waiting God often tells the human that waiting is the appropriate posture.

Many years before the birth of Jesus, the Old Testament prophets were writing and talking about waiting for one who would be like a light for the darkness. Those to whom they spoke were weary with impatience. They wanted the Messiah *now.* They yearned for God to be on their clock. For years added to more years, through the events of history, through priests and poets, God said, "Wait."

That same note is sounded in the prologue of John's Gospel. Those who gave ear to the preaching of John the Baptist heard him say, "I am not the light, but I come to tell you about the light that is yet to come" (John 1:8, AP). Dissatisfied with his lack of urgency, the listeners pressed him to say more, but John could only say, "I am not he." So anxious were they for a Messiah that the masses tried to crown John the Baptist as the Messiah. Again, God's message was "wait"....

The word *Advent* comes from the Latin word *advenire* (to come to). Advent's message is that God in Christ is coming to the world. This coming may be a past experience. God did come in Christ at Christmas. The prophets' promise was fulfilled in the Babe. This coming may also be a present experience. God may come to you this Christmas as a rebirth, either for the first time or as a renewed birth in the deeper regions of your being.

The Advent season, a period of four Sundays before Christmas Day, is a time of waiting for the Christian. This is an awkward season because it is most difficult for us to focus on the preliminary dimensions of the Christmas story. We had much rather go directly to Bethlehem without hearing anew the words of the prophets or John the Baptist. Advent does not give us permission to rush to the manger. It says "wait."

The mood of Adent is expressed in the liturgical color violet. The paraments of the sanctuary and the stoles of clergy are purple, depicting a feeling of quiet dignity, royalty, and repentance. Violet once was the traditional color of a king's robe. This color is used by the church to signal the coming of Christ who is the King of kings. Advent, a time of waiting, is a time of solemn and sober thought about one's need of repentance. It provides a quiet time for watching, waiting, and praying for a new experience of Christ's birth.

Advent is a time of solemnity and sobriety. Traditionally, Advent is a penitential season, originally known as the "Winter Lent." This mood of sobriety is expressed not only in the liturgical color, purple, but in the music of Advent hymns such as "O Come, O Come, Emmanuel" and "Come, Thou Long-Expected Jesus." In some parts of Christendom choirs omit processionals or have "silent processionals." Weddings are often discouraged. Decorations and things festive are often delayed until Christmas Eve.

Advent stresses not so much fulfillment as the anticipation of fulfillment: Christ is about to be born in the cradle of the believer's heart and life. As a family looks forward to a son returning from a war or a bride anticipates her wedding day, so a Christian looks forward with joy to Christ's coming. Yet, this is a different kind of joy—a joy of hope amid solemnity. It is the quiet joy of anticipation. . . .

There are two ways to wait during Advent. Some will wait with a hollow stare. Others will wait with anticipation. Knowing how to wait and where to look for Christ's coming is essential for the Advent season. People will look for Christ in a variety of places at this Advent. Some will look for his presence in the quiet visit of an old friend. Others will look for a sign of his coming in the reading of scripture, the thrill of a great novel, the majestic rhythm of an ageless poem, or in the sights, sounds, and symbols of congregational worship. Knowing how to wait and where to look is like a prelude to Messiah's birth.

—Joe E. Pennel, Jr.
*The Whisper of Christmas*

# A Litany for Those Who Wait

**Single Voice:** Frequently we are called to be a waiting people.

**Group:** We wait in traffic; we wait in stores, we wait for loved ones and friends.

**Single Voice:** At times we wait when we shouldn't.

**Group:** We know what needs to be done and we lack will.

**Single Voice:** Often we can do no more than wait; and our hearts become heavy from waiting.

**Group:** When life asks us to wait, may we feel your sustaining presence, O Lord!

**Single Voice:** Help us see the ministry of waiting with those who wait.

**Group:** Deliver us from aimless chatter and from fear of silence.

**Single Voice:** Grant us, O God, your sense of timing.

**Group:** Help us know when we sit back and when to move out.

**Single Voice:** We long for your word to break the uncertainty of our wait.

**Group:** We wait patiently for you, O Lord, for you hear our cry.

—Robert A. Noblett
*alive now!*

# The Holy Surprise

Read Luke 2:8–14.

How many Christmas pageants, manger scenes, musical compositions, or paintings, or poems, or stories have tried to pass on to us something of the astonishment, the wonder, the fear, the hope, that are described in this story of the shepherds on the hillside?

There they were tending their sheep, some of them probably dozing off, or thinking of what they would do when they got back home, or of how their children were, or their wives, or girl friends, or their parents. Nothing special going on.

And then, "Lo, the angel of the Lord came upon them, and the glory of the Lord shone round about them; and they were sore afraid" (KJV).

Who wouldn't be afraid? If you have been present when an eclipse of the sun makes important changes in the quality of light, you know how disorienting that can be—even when you knew it was going to happen!

But here, we are told, the fear didn't last. The message was one of incredible joy, or reassurance. What was the angel telling them? Of the birth of a baby? That they could understand, though this wasn't the usual mode of announcement. But a baby who was Christ the Lord? They were even told how to identify that baby!

And then, as though to add even greater authenticity to the message of the angel, came this multitude of the heavenly host, praising God and foretelling an era of peace—which, according to the Jewish counterpart of the word for peace, shalom, means full and complete life.

Had you been on the hillside, what would you have thought?

*PRAYER:* Glory to you, O God, in the highest. And on earth may there be peace. Amen.

—Martha Whitmore Hickman
*The Upper Room Disciplines 1986*

# Waiting

All my life I have waited: waited for the project to be completed, waited for supper to be ready, waited for the doctor to see me. I have waited at the traffic light, waited for the right relationship, waited to grow up.

I have waited alone or waited with friends. I have waited anxiously. I have waited expectantly. Some waits have brought joy. Other waits have brought bad news. Some waits have been "worth waiting for."

Now it is Advent, and I am waiting again. This time I am waiting in the darkness of my soul—ravaged by sorrow, anger, and fear. But I do not despair in the waiting, for I remember the way light looks and feels. The memories of silent nights with starlit skies are with me, and I have been bathed in the warmth of love's light. And so I hope—for Messiah to come.

Voices sing, "Prepare him room." I know now waiting cannot be passive. There is something to do, but where? I have no inn or stable, but in my heart, I can make room. Move over doubt. Move over despair. Make room for Truth, for Life, for Love. Make room for the Prince of Peace.

—**Kathy Clark-Dickens**
*alive now!*

# Wreathed in Flesh and Warm

It is unlike most other kinds of waiting. Certainly it is not like waiting for other anticipated events, even momentous ones: a long-awaited letter from a friend, a wedding day, a coveted job opportunity, the end of a painful illness. There is a quality, a texture to the waiting we do during pregnancy that is one only with the waiting we do for God.

That pregnancy and the entry of divine life into the world are inextricably related is, of course, at the heart of the Christian message. God became human in the person of Jesus through the person of Mary, through this woman's willingness to open herself, soul and body, to the divine seed that soon would flower for the redemption of the world. It was Mary's assent to the angel's startling announcement that ushered in a new age. It was in her pregnant womb that heaven and earth were so lovingly intermingled, through the waiting experienced in her flesh and blood that God was made to walk with humankind.

The majestic and cosmic implications of this unique pregnancy may fill us with an awe that separates us from intimate identification with what went on there. Yet there is a more personal dimension to that one creative event which does speak directly to each of us. Like the simple young woman in Nazareth, we may be surprised, at any time, by the intuition that we too are chosen. We are hailed to receive into ourselves the seed that God wishes to plant there. We say yes and the life of God begins its course of gestation in us. We become the ground out of which the incarnate God flowers in the world.

Mary's one unrepeatable pregnancy speaks to us of the life of the spirit growing within. This much we know. This much has been commented upon by Christian exegetes for centuries. But it is also true that each of our own pregnancies can speak to us of the direction of the divine wind moving in our world. For, if we are to take this incarnate God we worship seriously, we must come to learn that the wisdom of the created world, the wisdom of the body, is also the wisdom of the soul. There is grace at work in our blood and bones. There is divinity awaiting entry into human history at the threshold of our own hearts' doors.

Pregnancy is at the core of the Christian message. And so to gaze long and thoughtfully at the experience of pregnancy, especially as it is a process of waiting, is to learn something of the waiting we do for God, who breathes and moves in us, longing to be born. Perhaps being pregnant is so common an experience, so unconsciously connected to the self-identity of most women, that it may seem strange to look there for intimations of God's working in our hearts and in the world. Yet our Christian faith does not celebrate the reign of a disembodied deity but a God who is with us, a God whose presence here on earth, to use the phrase struck by poet Robert Stephen Hawker in his poem "Aisha Shekinah," is "wreathed in flesh and warm."[1]

Pregnancy is a time of waiting. It is, like the contemplative practice of the presence of God, a waiting that is also a "listening," a leaning inward toward the new life that is budding in the darkest center of one's being. I remember all three of my pregnancies as times of energy turned inwards, of what might have seemed a certain abstractedness or intimate preoccupation. In part this was simply a response to the biological fact that the creation of another person calls upon one's body to use all its available resources. Little energy is left over for outwardly directed activities. But the leaning inward of pregnancy takes place on another level, too, I would say. There is an attentiveness to the presence of another, a sensitivity to the cohabitation in time and space that is occurring within the deepest recesses of one's being. The other's presence is experienced in many different ways, which we shall explore; but there is an overarching sense of being in a different state throughout pregnancy. It is a sense of not being quite who you thought you were before. And the

---

[1]Robert Stephen Hawker, "Aisha Shekinah," found in *Anthology of Catholic Poets*, edited by Leslie Shane (Darby, PA: Arden Library, 1978.)

who you are coming to be has much to do with the life that is hidden inside.

Surrounding that unrevealed presence with one's questioning is part of the process of waiting. I am reminded of a statement made by a Trappist novice master I once met who, when asked about a life lived in Christian authenticity, responded that to be a Christian was not to know the answers but to begin to live in the part of the self where the question is born. He was, of course, not speaking about doubt concerning particular articles of faith but about a state of being. He was speaking of an attitude of listening, of awareness of presence, of an openness to mystery. A pregnant woman's questions encircling the seed inside her may come from many levels. They may involve wondering about the future child's sex, her own mothering capacities, its future rearing. But more deeply, the inarticulate questioning of pregnancy, that being present to the awesome and life-changing fact of the reality of new life, is like the age-old contemplative practice of the presence of God.

The consensus of many years of Christian prayer is that there is a presence into which we may enter. A presence that is unfailingly there. One of the most remarkable things about being pregnant, I remember, was the lived realization that, when one is pregnant, one is always pregnant. You wake up in the morning, move through the day, work, play, eat, love, and sleep pregnant. You cannot put it aside, take a vacation from it, and come back to it later. I am reminded of the story of Jonah and the intuition dramatized there that no matter where one runs, one cannot run away from God. For God is in the midst of us, in the very fabric of our lives. We can—Jonah-like—try to run away. We can fail, through the intentional or unintentional obstruction of our vision, to see the fact of the presence that is there. But it will pursue us and it will teach us its wisdom and direct us in its ways. Being pregnant, you are always pregnant. That fact pursues you and comes to inform everything you do.

Pregnancy is a contemplative time, a waiting like the waiting we do for God. In that waiting there are discernible rhythms which correspond to what I believe are two interrelated but distinctive processes. First, there is the rhythm of unfolding. To respond to this rhythm is to stay close to the hidden questioning going on within, listening to the answers that are not answers but that lead one deeper into the place of questioning. To be part of this rhythm of unfolding during pregnancy is to move quietly and inarticulately into the inward presence of another human person, to contemplate their personhood, to see their being through the eyes of God.

Waiting has yet another rhythm. This is the rhythm of the duration of the process, a journey which has a beginning, middle, and end. In each of our lives, God is gestated and born over and over again. And each time there is a birthing there has been a journeying process, an inner pilgrimage with a map all its own. Waiting during these journeys has many qualities, each of which corresponds to the segment of road on which we find ourselves at any given time. Not only is the waiting different at the start of a journey than at the end, but the identity of the pilgrim—the way we view ourselves and what we are about—changes along with the shifting landscapes. This self-identity, which, I believe, is linked to the unfolding quality of the waiting, occurs simultaneously with the changing process of the journey itself.

How different the identity of a pregnant woman in the first trimester of her pregnancy from the identity of a woman close to term—both for herself and for those around her. During the first few months a pregnancy may hardly reveal its full potential. It may seem as though what is happening at this point of the process is little related to what the end results will be. That early time may yield very few symptoms, perplexing the woman and making her want somehow to have confirmation of the fact of the life growing in her. How many women I have heard say (especially in their first pregnancy) that they couldn't wait "to show," to feel and look "really" pregnant. Or the first months may be a time of fatigue or debilitating nausea. It may hardly feel full of life or in communion with the creative capacities of God's world.

The first signs of presence are often unclear. There is during this time a longing for clarity, for confirmation, for a more embodied knowledge of what is with you. Yet there is no way to hurry the process, no easy remedy for discomfort or the lack of sign. In gestation waiting must be embraced. For there is nothing to do but wait. And the waiting of this early phase is, again, unlike most other waiting, for you are not waiting for the presence to go away but to show itself differently, to blossom into the visible statement of a swollen belly or to yield to the radiant surge of energy and the healthy glow of pinkened cheeks.

Yet in that invisible and sometimes tedious waiting, when your whole body does not yet proclaim who you are and what you are carrying, when the secret is hidden within the recesses of your inner space, when you alone, or only a few persons close to you know "the truth"—in that waiting there is an emergence of a new sort of question. Perhaps in many women it is not a question consciously asked. In some it is. The question is, "Who am I now that this surprising presence lives within me?" I think the answer is learned only over the long history of a lifetime, but its germ is present especially in the waiting of the early months. There is something, someone else who lives in me, to whom I am intimately linked. That someone, that intimacy, makes me someone different than I was before.

I have heard women in this first waiting time say, "I can't believe I'm actually going to have a baby, my own!" It is as if somehow the full reality of what is hinted at in the simple fact of being "barely pregnant" is glimpsed. Something very important is underway, and the present perception of it both lacks understanding yet grasps the momentous import of what is coming to be.

The contemporary phrase, descriptive of the state of God's kingdom in the world—"already but not yet"—is wondrously enfleshed in the waiting of the first months of pregnant life. So, too, it is in that other gestation of the spirit within each of us. We have opened ourselves to the seed of God's own life, perhaps through prayer or through the shock of a crisis or the influence of someone else. Now we wait, barely conscious that what is planted inside can and will bear fruit.

Our waiting on God is not simply passive, however; it is

active. God's life requires nurturing and attentive care in order for it to come to birth through us. The wisdom of our pregnant bodies tells us as much. I will never forget my amazement, the first time I was pregnant, at the fact that the gestation taking place asked so much of me. It was not only that I had to alter my accustomed routine but also that this emerging life became the focus of my whole person. It caught me up totally. My hormonal system shifted, my blood volume increased, the texture of my skin began to change, my gums became enflamed. I had a terrible craving for protein foods and an unavoidable need for long, deep periods of sleep. That little life within had taken control over the whole of myself, and its needs suddenly took priority over many otherwise necessary and interesting priorities.

I remember being amazed at the extent to which all this took place outside of my conscious control, at how much this female rite of passage was a larger and more primal process of which I was only one small part. That knowledge, that being caught up in the matrix of creation itself, deepened my sense of question, "Who am I?" I asked. "How am I different now that I see myself from the perspective of this primal human/divine process that is gestation and, ultimately, birth?"

This sense of being caught up with the whole self, of being asked actively to nurture what is growing within, is a characteristic of the spiritual life as well. We do not simply assent to God's presence; we incarnate it. It comes to be through the longing of our hearts and the labors of our bodies. It comes at the expense of the very life that courses through our veins.

God is born in time. Yet at the meeting of divine and human, time is also timeless. It is this quality of waiting that, for me, characterized the second phase of my pregnancies. The unseen was by this time beginning to be seen, the sense of "just being sick" was giving way to renewed energy and health. And the miracle of what was happening was slowly beginning to dawn on me. The restless perplexity of the first trimester was gone, but I had not yet entered the later period when the sense of imminence was heightened. I was just waiting.

Visibly pregnant with that gently rounded contour that is still manageable and not yet heavy with the ripeness of the last months, I experienced the eternal quality of the life of God within. It was as though this secret within me, to which my continual if unfocused attention was drawn by its very incarnateness, was leading me to a dark and hidden realm of existence. Here I was, at the first moment of creation, at the imperceptible moment when what had been nothing was suddenly something, when—at God's bidding—the unstirred was stirred. I was in the realm of God's own mysterious life force where beginning and ending become fused in a totality of meaning, where out of no time a finite human life erupted into the stream of history and began its pilgrimage.

Simply being during this time was miraculous, especially during my first pregnancy when I had the leisure (because I did not have other small children) to reflect on the experience and to respond to the pressing need for rest and proper nourishment. It was contemplative waiting during these months, a dawning awareness of the still center within which the human person opens out onto the divine life. Being was rich and infused with stillness, informing my continuing question, "Who am I now?" I began to have a sense of what is meant when we who are parents are referred to as co-creators with God.

Yet, the sense of the timelessness of the waiting does not characterize all of a pregnancy. The waiting can be very hard. In part, this is because the waiting is for something, not simply an end in itself. What is hidden wants to come to light. What is gestating wants to be born. And we press forward in anticipation, longing to know, to touch, to hold, to see, to name. In the classic spirituality of Ignatius Loyola this longing—the desire of the human heart—is seen as both a prerequisite for and the central dynamic of the life in God. In Ignatius's view it is our deepest desires that point us toward the ultimate object of our longings—toward God and the fulfillment of our hearts. There is, then, in the waiting upon God an element of restlessness, an intuition of incompletion which goads us to question, to discern. The waiting is not passive but catches us up in its inner dynamism. So too, a waiting pregnant woman aches to finally hold her child in her arms and call it by name. Her desire is for the issue of the vital process occurring within.

Waiting can be hard for another reason. The pregnancy may be fraught with discomfort and inconvenience; it may be attended by anxiety of many kinds; it may be dangerous, life-threatening to either the woman or the child. This is especially true of the last trimester when, even under the best of circumstances, the strength and size of the developing life within impinges on a woman's being in a way that is often difficult. Backaches, varicose veins, swollen ankles, high blood pressure, sleep difficulties, fears about the health of the child, anxiety about the impending birth, uncertainty about the community, the world into which this child comes— all these may make the waiting hard.

The fears, the pains are real. They are part of the stuff of the miraculous waiting. They speak to us, they embody for us the truth that there is no new life without a dying, no effortless way to be part of the creative process operative in this, our God's world. We do not give life without giving of our own lives. So, too, we do not bring God's spirit to birth without suffering, without giving out of the very substance of who we are. This hardness of the waiting, in both spiritual and physical pregnancy, speaks to us of another face of the incarnate divine life that we celebrate. There is a darkness to our God, a suffering and dying visage, that we sometimes choose to ignore. It is not easy to ignore the pains of physical pregnancy. But we do recoil from spiritual darkness both in ourselves and as it is manifest in our world.

Yet our bodies tell us, as do the symbols of our Christian faith, that suffering with the pain, being part of it, is what we must do. For in that pain, that shameful vision of our dying God, we begin to experience the answer to our most urgent human questions. We begin to understand communion, compassion, and participatory love. We begin to enter into the life that God intended for us, a life in which we live out the profound interconnectedness of us all. This life is symbolized for us in our Paschal Lord. It is also embodied in a woman's flesh.

What pregnant woman does not have a body-knowledge, perhaps only unconsciously appreciated, of the intimate connectedness of all life? What pregnant woman does not have some sense of the blood that invisibly flows between us, a torrent whose waters course unchecked through our own veins, through the veins of our children and our children's children, whose waters came to us through our own mother's swollen body?

A pregnant woman is not simply a self, a discreet entity maneuvering deftly among other discreet selves. She is bound, at the most intimate center of her being, to another being. She is linked, blended by the tissues of her body, to another life. Through the hardness of the waiting of pregnancy—a hardness that exists because of the shared quality of being in the waiting—she knows the sweet yet costly truth of the interconnectedness of all life.

The question evolving through the process of pregnancy— "Who am I?"—comes to be answered this way: "I am a somebody whose life is intimately and for all times connected to another life, and through that life, to all other lives." I think of that curious and touching communion of pregnant women I discovered with great surprise the first time I was pregnant. The body wisdom I discovered there identified me with all those named and nameless women who had for nine months been at the center of creation, the center of the web of life: I was initiated, too, by my physical coexistence with another person, into the communion of blood and water that binds all life together. And I became intimate with the timeless moment at which the creator and the created meet, conscious of the still point inside the life that I am where new life is born.

The wisdom of the body is the wisdom of the soul. Divine life is encoded in human flesh. We wait for God's life to grow in us, to enter the world. The waiting can be hard. We can be spent in the process. The spending can impinge upon us in ways we could never have imagined. It may feel as though the

41

marrow of our bones is being sucked out, as though we must die before God can be born through us. But the mystery we live is that our suffering is also a new birth. There is really one greater and more generous life of which we are one part. Our being born into it, our allowing it to come through us, is part of the creative and redemptive process of our God.

Pregnancy is at the core of the Christian message. We are pregnant. We are the place of waiting, the place of the question, of the advent. We are the womb through whose pulsing life God is born.

—Wendy M. Wright
*Weavings*

# Emmanuel

Read Isaiah 9:6–7

The virgin will conceive and bear a son, and he shall be called "Emmanuel", a name which means "God is with us."
—Matthew 1:23 (NEB)

On Christmas Eve, I sat weeping in a hospital waiting room. Our daughter's baby was coming too soon, and there was danger for her and for the child.

After a few moments, a woman moved across the room to sit by my side. She asked why I was crying, and, with relief, I poured out my worries and fears to her. Soon, we were talking together like old friends. My fears were forgotten for a while.

In time, the woman was called away; her grandchild had been born. As she left the room, she turned to me and said, "Remember, God is with us."

On Christmas morning, our granddaughter was born safely. As the family rejoiced, I thought of the kind woman and the help she had given me. The memory of her sweet face comes to me often. She not only knew the meaning of the word *Emmanuel;* she knew how to share it.

*PRAYER:* Creator, we thank you for the witnesses you send to us when we need them the most. May we in turn share our faith and strength with someone who needs to be reminded of your love and care. Amen.

THOUGHT FOR THE DAY

Our knowledge of the constant presence of God allows us to face any situation with courage.

—Billye Reed (Tennessee)
*The Upper Room*

# The Ministry of Waiting

Read Psalm 105:16–24

God sent me ahead of you to preserve for you a remnant on earth and to save your lives by a great deliverance.
—Genesis 45:7 (NIV)

Joseph waited year after painful year in Egypt—twenty years, in all—before he saw his dreams come true. The time spent in Potiphar's house, then in prison, must have seemed not only incredibly long but also wasted. There seemed to be no connection between these experiences and the dream God gave Joseph when he was a boy.

So, too, God often gives us a vision for our future. But like Joseph's circumstances, ours may seem far removed from what we would like to see happen.

During this time, God gives us the ministry of waiting. They are hard years. We feel nothing is being accomplished. Our prayers don't seem to be answered. And more, waiting is just plain difficult.

Yet Joseph's years in Egypt were raw material for his ministry. He learned the language; he learned administration and leadership. Did he understand what God was doing? Perhaps not. But God sent Joseph to Egypt to save his family from future famine.

Like Joseph, we can make use of the responsibilities we have now and leave God to work out the answer in God's time.

*PRAYER:* Lord, thank you for my dreams. Thank you for today's tasks, because they, too, are part of your plan. Amen.

THOUGHT FOR THE DAY

God is preparing me today for my future.

—Sandi Somers (Canada)
*The Upper Room*

# *Two*

## Gifts

*Opening their treasures,*
*[the wise men] offered [Jesus]*
*gifts of gold, frankincense, and myrrh.*

Matthew 2:11, RSV

*[All who believe] are justified*
*by [God's] grace as a gift,*
*through the redemption*
*which is in Christ Jesus.*

Romans 3:24, RSV

# To Learn from the Poor

Read James 2:1–9

Has not God chosen those who are poor in the world to be rich in faith and heirs of the kingdom which he has promised to those who love him?                    —James 2:5 (KJV)

I had been invited to speak at a church in the Midwest shortly before Christmas. Another minister from the area asked if I would speak at his small rural church earlier the same Sunday.

That morning the temperature was nineteen below zero. The rural community was extremely poor. Many homes had no indoor plumbing, and many had outer walls covered only with tar paper.

The church was crowded and the service heartwarming. But there was a little girl on the front row who glowed with joy. Her eyes dancing, her feet constantly moving, she was listening, singing, and praying. I could not keep my eyes off her. She was no more than six years old, and she was dressed shabbily. She wore socks on her hands because she had no mittens, and she had walked a quarter of a mile to church.

After the service I asked her about Christmas. She simply said, "All I'll get is what I get here." But she said it joyfully.

*PRAYER:* Dear God, we hurt for those who do not have what they need. Help us to share with them and learn from them. Amen.

THOUGHT FOR THE DAY

All of us have much to learn from those who have little to give.

—Tom H. Matheny (Louisiana)
*The Upper Room*

# Let Me Not Keep Christmas

Let me not
wrap
stack
box
bag
tie
tag
bundle
seal
KEEP
Christmas.

Christmas kept
is liable to mold.

Let me give Christmas away
unwrapped
by exuberant armfuls.
Let me
share
dance
LIVE
Christmas
unpretentiously
merrily
responsibly
with overflowing hands
tireless step
and sparkling eyes.
Christmas given away
will stay fresh—
even until it comes again.

—Linda Felver
*alive now!*

# The First Christmas Card

As we all know, the giving of Christmas cards is a tradition. But did you ever wonder why? Well, I am here to tell you.

Back in Bible times, people didn't have Christmas cards. They didn't even have Christmas! They didn't know that Christmas was coming that year. The angel told Mary about the coming child.

Well, the angel Gabriel was the first Christmas card. And who gave the card? God.

Well, that's the story of the first Christmas card!

—Anne Louise Miller, age 11
*alive now!*

# The Greatest Gift of All

## *A Children's Story*

It was Christmastime in a village far away. Angelica was so excited about the celebrations of Jesus' birth that she wanted everyone to know that *the Christ Child is the greatest gift of all!*

The whole village was hustling and bustling getting ready for Christmas. People were decorating trees, buying gifts for everyone on their lists, giving big parties, and preparing big dinners. Nobody—but nobody—had time to notice a little girl.

Angelica's mother was baking cookies when Angelica tugged at her skirt to tell her new discovery. "Mama, the Christ Child is the greatest gift of all!"

"Not now, dear," her mother said absent-mindedly.

Angelica saw her neighbor bringing in a sack of toys for his children, so she rushed outside to tell him her good news. "Sir," she said, quite politely, "the Christ Child is the greatest gift of all!"

"Run along now, miss," came the gruff reply.

None of the villagers had time to stop to pay any attention to Angelica's good news, and Angelica became discouraged. *No one will listen to me,* she thought.

Then, on the day before Christmas, she had an idea! She tied bits of colored yarn on little bells and walked all through her village. As the grown-ups paused to chat or as people stopped to look in store windows or to wait for a carriage to cross the street, Angelica pinned a bell on a cuff or a hem and whispered ever so gently, "The Christ Child is the greatest gift of all!"

It was the tiniest of whispers. People hardly even thought about it at the time.

At midnight on Christmas Eve the village gathered for the

great celebration in the square. The jingling of little bells became louder and merrier as everyone in the village came.

A little girl danced with delight around the giant village Christmas tree. It was Angelica!

And without ever knowing where the idea came from, everyone smiled because they knew: THE CHRIST CHILD IS THE GREATEST GIFT OF ALL!

You, like Angelica, can remind everyone around you that Christmas is really all about Jesus and his birth. With tiny safety pins and scraps of yarn, you can turn little jingle bells into a good news message for everyone.

Thread the yarn through the bells and tie a bow. Then put a pin through the yarn. Write on a slip of paper, "Jesus is the greatest gift of all" and put the slip of paper on the pin. As you carefully pin these on your friends, remind them that the Christ Child is the greatest gift of all! Whenever they wear the bell and hear it jingle, they will be reminded.

—Wineva Hankamer
*Pockets*

# It Is a Gift

Read Ephesians 2:1–10

It is by [God's] grace you are saved. . . . It is God's gift, not a reward for work done. —Ephesians 2:8–9 (NEB)

One day I heard a mother tell how her young son worked through three quarters of a football game gathering soft-drink bottles in order to pay her back for the price of his admission ticket.

"We didn't want him to work during the game," she said sadly. "We wanted him to enjoy it." She was obviously torn between hurt for the child's missed enjoyment and bewildered appreciation for his efforts.

She said, "I'll never forget his sweaty little face as he told me he lacked only two bottles before he could pay us back. His father and I had thought all the time that he was enjoying the ballgame with his friends."

We relate to God that way much of the time. We work and sweat and strain to pay God back for the gifts of life and love when God wants us to relax and live our lives fruitfully. God wants only our love.

PRAYER: Dear God, help me to accept your gifts and to show my gratitude by loving you and others. I pray as Jesus taught, "Our Heavenly Father, may your name be honored; May your kingdom come, and your will be done on earth as it is in Heaven. Give us this day the bread we need, Forgive us what we owe to you, as we have also forgiven those who owe anything to us. Keep us clear of temptation, and save us from evil."* Amen.

THOUGHT FOR THE DAY
Peace comes from the acceptance of God's grace.

—Dorothy C. Potts (Georgia)
*The Upper Room*

*Matthew 6:9–13 (Phillips).

# Christmas Cookies

A little child shall lead them.　　　—Isaiah 11:6 (RSV)

Mr. Baker was a grouch. All the neighborhood children said so. Our older boys used to fight with his children—nothing serious, just bickering back and forth. But he told a mutual friend that our children were brats and that he didn't like our family.

Along with our teenagers, we had a three-year-old child, Brian. For some reason Brian had always liked Mr. Baker and even helped him work in his yard. He called him his "buddy." When Christmas rolled around Brian wanted to bake cookies and decorate them. "Mommy, I'd like to take a plate of my cookies to Mr. Baker." I tried to discourage him. "Please, Mom," Brian had said. "We're pals." I gave in.

We placed the cookies on a paper plate, covered them with foil, and put a ribbon on the top. I watched as Brian was greeted by Mr. Baker, who grinned as he took the cookies, dispelling my apprehension.

As I stood at the door, he yelled "Merry Christmas" and waved. "God bless," I yelled back. These were the first words spoken between us in seven years.

Isn't that what Christmas is all about?

*PRAYER*: Thank you, God, for little children. Please make us aware of the ways in which they can lead us to Christ. Amen.

THOUGHT FOR THE DAY

The ways of a child can strengthen our faith.

—Pat Stackhouse (Indiana)
*The Upper Room*

53

# Faith in Action

Read James 2:8–18

Truly, I say to you, as you did it to one of the least of these . . . , you did it to me.     —Matthew 25:40 (RSV)

Juan Carlos, a lanky youth from a poor barrio, is justifiably proud that he has overcome his addiction to drugs. He recently discovered a receptive community here in our little church in Arroyito. For several months, Juan Carlos has been attending church regularly, to find a spirituality that will sustain him.

The winters here are cold and damp, and one member of our church noticed that Juan Carlos was shivering from the cold. When she learned that he did not have a warm coat, she gave him her second coat, a unisex mackinaw that just fit.

He carries this coat with him even on warm days now. It has become for him a symbol of the care and warmth of the Christian faith. This loving act of a concerned person has helped to bring about a transformation in Juan Carlos' life.

We all need to become more sensitive to the basic spiritual and material needs of the persons around us. A loving gesture to meet a need can have transforming power, for the recipient and for the giver.

*PRAYER:* Dear Lord, make us more aware of the persons around us and their needs. Show us how to reach out to them in wisdom and love. Amen.

THOUGHT FOR THE DAY
A loving heart can warm another's soul.

—Ray and Delaine DeHainaut (Santa Fe, Argentina)
*The Upper Room*

# The Days of Didymus

Gifting is a way to demonstrate love. It requires that we study another so intensely as to perceive his or her unspoken desires and meet them. It means to startle with the unexpected, perfectly chosen. For our children we have always seen it as a way to form a thankful and satisfied adult, to create a readiness for generosity, the early habits of appreciation, and a sense of blessedness.

But already I am defeated, for I can accomplish only so much of this and no more. I go back up the hill and through the fence into the yard sure that this Christmas I'll make a wrong selection, disappoint one of the children beyond the limits of his or her vulnerability, lose God's voice as I have lost God's creatures, be too weary to worship.

All of which is to say that there is immeasurable risk involved in Christmas, whether the popular pulpit wants to admit it or not. In many ways I suspect, like St. Thomas, that the days from the Joseph candle to the midnight service on Christmas Eve have very little to do with Jesus or Wise Men or salvation in the minds and attentions of most of us. But they do have a great deal to do with the soul's education.

In all that stress of bearing up under my own limitations and of exposing my failures to those I love; in all that searching to understand the next name on the list well enough to buy something that will be reasonably near where he or she really is in life; in all that yearning to continue creating good things inside our children, knowing the process has grown beyond my reach—in all that, there is not only the sense of doubt and impotence but also there is always the sense of release that comes at ten o'clock on Christmas Eve.

At our house nowadays, the gifts are opened by then. In earlier days they weren't opened until Christmas, but the effect is the same. Going out the door toward midnight service I always, invariably and blessedly, feel that relaxation which says it is done, that this one event in which we integrate and inter-react with each other more intensely than at any other time has reached its climax. Tomorrow we can go back to living together again, each of us as ourselves, and quit for another year trying to project into each other's wants and needs and desires. We can go back to the simple knowledge that in giving and receiving we have been involved at the deepest level of intimacy, have failed in places and succeeded in others. We have stopped to know each other in the stillness of the winter with no help outside ourselves, no impetus, no motivation beyond our own will to make holy the day for our God.

It has always seemed to me worth remembering that Christmas, while it is the high festival of the church, is also the only holy day we routinely celebrate in the dark of the night. And that the good man honored in those harsh days from the Joseph candle to the midnight mass is indeed St. Thomas the Doubter, old Didymus himself. I have long suspected the ancient church fathers who assigned functions and places in the liturgical calendar of a deep, if somewhat wry, wisdom. Certainly every year in the middle of that service when the Host is elevated and the first "Hosanna" rises from the choir loft, I can say with Thomas, "My Lord and my God!" (John 20:28). And each year that has made all the difference.

—Phyllis A. Tickle
*What the Heart Already Knows*

# The Red Cup

## *A Children's Story*

Judy was sitting alone in her room, with the snow swirling around outside. Soon she must go down and sit with her grandmother—her great-grandmother, really, though they had always laughed about her being great and grand, both.

Now Judy shivered a little as she thought of her, sitting in her wheelchair and not saying a word. That was what bothered Judy most. Always before she and her grandmother had had all kinds of things to talk about—the presents she was making for Mom and Dad, the Christmases when Grandma had been a little girl, the time Grandpa had given her the red cup.

But since Grandma had come from the hospital, she didn't say anything—not anything. She had tried once or twice when she first came to live there, but the words didn't come out right. Now she wouldn't try any more.

"Judy," her mother said quietly, opening the door. She had her coat and boots on ready for the last day's shopping before Christmas. "Judy, I'm going now. Your grandmother is all right, but go in and talk to her in a little while. The doctor says that may help."

She gave Judy a quick hug. "I know it's hard, dear; but just tell her something you're doing in school, or what we're planning for Christmas Eve. Bye, now." Her mother was gone.

Judy sat there, thinking what she would talk about. Christmas Eve! It would not be the same without the red cup. On Christmas Eve Grandma had always let her have her eggnog in the red cup.

Now they didn't even know where it was. When Grandma had come to live with them, her furniture and dishes had been sold. The other things had been packed in a hurry, but nobody even remembered seeing the red cup.

It wasn't all red. The bottom of it and the handle were clear glass, cut in little diamonds, but the top was bright red, with *Judith* written in clear glass and the date, 1914—the year Grandma had been married. She and Grandpa had gone to the fair, and he had bought the cup at a little booth there. He had had her name and the date put on it and given it to her. But where was it now?

Judy jumped up and started for the door. Then she turned back and picked up the play she was learning a part in for Christmas. She would read that out loud. Grandma would have read the other parts for her before, but at least it was something to do.

"Hi, Grandma," she said, as she went in. "I've got to learn a part for the Christmas play, so I brought it to read to you."

Her grandmother looked at her, but said nothing. She didn't smile; she just looked. Judy opened the book quickly and tried to find her place. It was as if Grandma weren't living anymore; she was just watching other people live. Judy blinked away the tears and started reading.

All the next day was a rush. Judy helped her mother make fudge, wrap the last presents, get out the best dishes. She washed and wiped the special glasses they would all have their eggnog in before the first presents were opened that night. She wondered who would be drinking out of the red cup or whether it had been broken and thrown away.

Under the tree they put the packages Grandma had wrapped before she was sick. They had tried to ask her whom they were for, but she had just turned her head away.

At last everything was ready. Judy's father had gotten home early. Her older sister and her husband had come for supper, and now the dishes were all cleared away. Grandma had been wheeled in by the tree, and they were all settling down in their favorite places when Judy's mother came in with the eggnog glasses on the Christmas tray. Judy and the others began to sing, "Here we come a-wassailing." Her mother stopped in front of grandmother for her to take the first glass.

She looked at the tray, and suddenly everyone saw a difference. She was not just staring at the tray; she was really looking. They stopped singing. Her mouth began to move. It looked as if she was talking, but there was no sound. She tried again. This time she did speak out loud. It was not very clear, but Judy understood.

" 'Red cup' she is saying," Judy exclaimed. "She wants the red cup!"

Nobody else said a word. How could they tell her, especially on Christmas Eve, that the red cup was gone?

Judy's mother set the tray on a side table and knelt beside the wheelchair. She started to explain, but grandmother shook her head and pointed to the tree. "Ju—dith," her voice cracked, but they all heard it. "Ju—dith's . . . red . . . cup." She leaned forward.

Quickly Judy's father pushed her chair closer to the tree. She leaned over to point at a package wrapped in red tissue. Judy's father picked it up and laid it on her lap.

"Do you think . . . ?" whispered Judy's mother.

Grandmother kept her hands on the box and said again, "Ju—dith."

Hardly daring to breathe, Judy came to stand beside her grandmother's chair. Her grandmother lifted the package. Judy glanced at her father, and he nodded. Carefully she took it from her grandmother, peeled back the wrapping and opened the box. "Oh!" she gasped.

There it was: the shining red cup, with *Judith 1914* on its side! Tears began to run down Judy's face as she looked at her grandmother. But Grandma was smiling!

"Mer—ry . . . Christ—mas," she said, before she was quite swallowed up in Judy's big hug.

—Edith E. Cutting
*Pockets*

# Christmas Day

**Read 2 Corinthians 4:1–6**

God loved the world so much that he gave his only Son, so that everyone who believes in him may not die but have eternal life. —John 3:16 (TEV)

Some of my wooden soldiers are missing. My father gave away those highly decorated soldiers on Christmas morning, 1945. I remember with pain my first lesson in sharing.

On that Christmas morning we children were opening our gifts in the splendor that parents seem to create on Christmas morning. A knock came at the door, and I could see our neighbors Wayne and Kate standing on the porch looking through the frost-coated window.

"Come on in," bellowed my father. "Come and join us." Two neighborhood children had interrupted our extravaganza. "Hey, Wayne," I yelled, "what did you get for Christmas?" In a very quiet voice came the reply from Wayne, "Nothing. Santa lost his way and missed our house."

The festive room suddenly became very quiet. All of us realized that our visitors had missed Christmas gifts of their own. We all knew their family was struggling to survive. The father had abandoned the home many years before. The mother was trying desperately hard to keep her family together. There was nothing left for the extras of Christmas.

My father broke the silence. "Hey, kids, Santa did get lost and left your gifts at our house." I knew instantly that some of my soldiers were going to sleep in another home that night. Without another word, my parents started picking their way through some of our gifts and handing them to Wayne and Kate.

The joy and laughter in their faces will always remain in my memory. I found it hard to understand everything at the time, but my father explained everything later in the day. On my tenth Christmas I discovered the meaning of sharing.

I really don't know where Wayne and Kate are today, but I'll never forget my father's love and my mother's grace so many years ago. At Christmas we share the good news by the giving of gifts. The shepherds brought their sheep to the manger and the wise men brought gifts of gold, frankincense, and myrrh. What gifts will we give this Christmas to celebrate God's gift of himself to us?

*PRAYER:* God, our Father, we thank you for giving us life, and for teaching us that to give is to live. Empower us to show your love by loving those of your children who share the same time and space with us. We pray in the name of Jesus Christ. Amen.

THOUGHT FOR THE DAY

At Christmas we share the good news by the giving of gifts—the greatest of which is ourselves.

—Douglas S. Miller (Montclair, New Jersey)
*The Upper Room*

# Send 'Em a Check

Dear Christine,

The first cold tendrils of reality have brushed against my New Year's resolution [to make Christmas a Christ-centered celebration.] We had the bazaar worknight last night, and I had a game plan all ready. I was going to offer them a fat check and then check out.

All I could think about was the time that would now be available to me, time that had previously been spent crocheting pink poodles and making plastic Dixie cup bells. I would have whole hours in which to contemplate the true meaning of Christmas. I envisioned myself in meaningful meditation, undisturbed by the guilt of unfinished pine cone wreaths. Opting out of the bazaar would be my first strike for a Christian Christmas.

I never even got to first base. The check is still in my purse, right beside the pattern for a tree ornament made from margarine tub tops. (Enclosed with this letter—I thought you might like it for your bazaar.)

As you know, Chris, I am not an avid meeting attender. In fact, on a list of things I'd like to do, I'd rate cleaning the bathtub or grooming the dog before going to a meeting. So, it was with some reluctance that I agreed to go to the worknight. Actually, the reason I went stems from when I was a teenager. I was always the one who wouldn't break up with a boyfriend over the phone, thinking it more humane to do it face-to-face, and I suppose it was a similar kind of thinking that made me attend the meeting. Just sending in a check would have been easier but more cowardly.

Chris, have you ever had the feeling that somebody up there has set you up? You know, that feeling that everything that happens is divinely planned to speak to you. Do you occasionally hear the angels chuckling at your expense? That's how it was at the worknight.

Even though the meeting was meant to be a working session, we still had to attend to the formalities: roll call, scripture reading, meditation, prayer, and hymn. Mrs. Baine, our president, called the meeting to order and asked us to name our favorite Christmas carol, "just to put us in the right mood for the evening." She asked me to start.

Well, I was ready to let them have it. I'd not only give them a carol title, but also a small speech on my new attitude toward Christmas. It didn't quite work out the way I had planned.

Occasionally, much to my embarrassment, I forget words, names of people, and things. Once I even forgot Gerald's name when I was introducing him to some friends. Well, it happened again. Only this time, I forgot the name of a Christmas carol. You're not going to believe this, Christine, but the only title I could think of was "Jingle Bells." I suppose it could have been worse. I suppose "Rudolph, the Red-Nosed Reindeer" or "Santa Claus Is Coming to Town" might have caused a bigger stir, but I doubt it. I made some inane remark about being a part of today's Christmas world, but I don't think they bought it. Somehow, the moment wasn't right to make my "freedom" speech.

Mrs. Clark gave a brief meditation. Now, usually I can count on Mrs. Clark to read something light, often a rhyming verse with a cute twist of phrase at the end. But this evening she dove into Oswald Chambers's book *My Utmost for His Highest*. The topic was "The Worship of the Work," and one line really struck home. It was, "There is no responsibility on you for the work; the only responsibility you have is to keep in living, constant touch with God, and to see that you allow nothing to hinder your cooperation with Him." Ouch! About this time, I began to wish that I'd just broken up over the phone; that is, sent the check and stayed home.

It got worse. Mrs. Bellows handed out our memory verse for the evening, Ecclesiastes 9:10: "Whatsoever thy hand findeth to do, do it with thy might." I pinned mine onto a shrinking heart.

The closing hymn was the clincher: "Take My Life, and Let It Be Consecrated." I was finished. I mentally said goodbye to those blissfully free hours and prepared myself to accept the responsibility for ten toilet roll covers, six tree ornaments, four pairs of mittens, two dozen cookies, an afternoon of sorting, an afternoon of selling, and an afternoon of clearing up at the bazaar.

Our spiritual food dispensed with, we got down to the real business of the evening. Mrs. Bellows handed out patterns for various ornaments. Mrs. Clark demonstrated some of the trickier versions. Mrs. Baine showed us some new slipper variations, and we all tried our hand at the margarine tub top angels. (Actually, mine turned out pretty well.)

You'll be pleased to know that I had several requests for the poodle pattern. Perhaps we should consider marketing these things ourselves. I bet we could think of a lot more things that could be covered by poodles: teapots, pencil holders, garbage cans, television sets—why the possibilities are endless! We could build a marketing empire based on poodles; we could start a whole new trend in home decorating; we could be as big as pink flamingos. But, I digress.

The meeting ended with a display of some of the work our members had already done. There was the usual stuff: knitted slippers, mittens, oven gloves, place mats, tea cosies—most with Santa motifs, or at least a sprinkling of holly and poinsettias. Audrey Cleary, however, had made the most beautiful wildflower stationery. She had dried flowers and pressed them between clear sheets, and then glued them onto writing paper. They were exquisite. Every one was different, and I kept thinking of how much time she had spent on each arrangement.

From Show-and-Tell time, we launched into a spirited discussion on pricing. Mrs. Baine always aims for the low side. "That way, we'll be sure to sell everything, and we won't be left with a lot of junk on our hands." On the other end of the scale, Mrs. Candy, our treasurer, is out to make our fortune. "People like to spend money at the bazaar. After all, everyone knows it's for a good cause. Let's take in as much as we can." Who can argue with logic like that?

In the end, the bottom line was the cost of the materials, so we priced accordingly. Two dollars' worth of wool meant a two-dollar ticket on the item. There was no markup for labor or skill or originality.

I put my hand in my purse to pull out the check. I'd still rather just pay the price and have my freedom.

I looked over at Audrey Cleary and wondered how she felt, having her beautiful work offered at bargain-basement prices. Without thinking, I said, "How much would your stationery be worth at a gift shop, Audrey? That is, if they paid you for your time and your skill?"

Audrey smiled at me. I noticed how tired she looked. No wonder: three children under seven, a big house, and, ever since her husband hurt his back, all the farm work to be done. How on earth had she ever found time for her handicrafts?

"I don't count time and skill," she said. She looked a little embarrassed, and I wished I'd kept my thoughts to myself. "The way I see it, they both come from the Lord, and since that's who I'm working for when I'm making things for the bazaar, well, I can hardly charge for them, can I?" She carefully tidied up her sheets of paper and, without looking at any of us, said, "I like to make things for the bazaar. I pray over each and every item, and I like to think that when someone buys something, they buy a prayer as well." She laughed softly. "For the Christmas bazaar, I always pray that the person will find Christ in their Christmas. It's kind of fun, picturing some absolute stranger benefiting from my prayer."

I put my check away, picked up my pattern for the margarine-tub-top angel, and came home.

Today, I started knitting the first pair of mitts. You know, Christine, it is fun, just as Audrey said. I pictured some small child receiving them, perhaps as a Christmas present, and then I prayed special things for that child. The time that I had earlier resented giving up became a time with the Lord. I was wrapped in meaningful meditation, contemplating the true meaning of Christmas, just as I had wanted to be.

I can hardly wait to start on the pink poodles—they are going to need some special prayer!

Must go now. My knitting needles call.

Love and a hug all around,

Pat

—Patricia Wilson
*Too Much Holly, Not Enough Holy?*

# The Coming Christ

Read Matthew 1:21–25; John 3:16–17

The coming Christ is our Savior. In a dream, Joseph was told to give Mary's baby the name Jesus. This was a common name in biblical times. Meaning "Yahweh is salvation," it gave each Jewish family who chose it the hope that their child would be the long-awaited messiah. By instructing Joseph to use the name, God was reaffirming Jesus' mission as Savior of the world.

The Jewish people expected a Savior who would deliver them from their earthly struggles. Today, many Christians want the same type of deliverance. We want material blessings and a general elimination of all our problems. But Jesus didn't come into the world to give us an easy life. He came to save us from our real problem—alienation from God. Jesus Christ came to deliver the best gift anyone can offer, eternal life with God.

Make a mental list of what people fear most today—nuclear war, famine, economic disaster. Add a list of the worst things that could happen to you personally. Then read Revelation 21 and 22. Stack the list you made against the description of our eternal life in heaven. This is the life Jesus came to save us for.

Jesus wants to help us with our daily problems, and he offers us power to conquer the sin in our lives. However, Christ's role is not limited to this world. Daily burdens cannot overwhelm us. Remember, we are being preserved by Christ for an eternity with God.

*Prayer:* Jesus, thank you for the priceless gift of salvation and the joy of an eternity with you. Amen.

—Jeanette Strong
*The Upper Room Disciplines 1986*

# The Gift of Self

Read John 10:7–10

The Word was the source of life, and this life brought light to mankind.                                      —John 1:4 (TEV)

She lived alone in a mobile home in an area of Miami that many people considered dangerous. She was about to celebrate her 99th Christmas.

A well-dressed man carrying a poinsettia arrived at her door on the afternoon before Christmas. With great caution she demanded to know who was there. She was surprised to discover that it was her doctor, for she was used to seeing him in a white coat. With a smile that brushed away most of her wrinkles, she invited him in for a chat and cup of coffee.

When I visited her the next day, she told me about the event of this special visitor with so beautiful a gift. With mellow, joyous restraint, she said, "Pastor, he didn't send the gift, he brought it himself!"

How well she expressed the Incarnation—God coming into our hearts and lives. And God's gift was very God! As John expressed it in his Gospel, this life brought light to everyone.

*PRAYER:* Eternal Love, thank you for coming in person with life's greatest gift. Amen.

THOUGHT FOR THE DAY

God is willing to come to every heart in person.

—Lee R. VanSickle (Florida)
*The Upper Room*

# Three

## Hope, Mystery, and Love

*Sing, heavens! Shout for joy, earth!*
  *Let the mountain burst into song!*
*The Lord will comfort his people;*
  *he will have pity on his suffering people.*

Isaiah 49:13, TEV

# The Recovery of Celebration

It is easy to hate Christmas. Although it may be the best season for some, for many it is the worst. Most of these individuals do not even know how large a company they keep. For many, one of the worst things about Christmas is that it is a season of so much celebration! The celebration gap between the happy and the sad tends to grow wider during Advent and Christmas than at any other time of the year. As the spirits of some people soar, the spirits of others, instead of soaring, tend to diminish and to depress. When all you feel like doing is crying, it hurts deeply to be expected to laugh.

*What is there to celebrate*
*in the midst of affluence, if you are poor?*
*in the midst of family reunions, when you are alone?*
*in the midst of love, when you feel rejected?*

*What is there to celebrate*
*about the sparkling eyes of children when you are*
*trying to deal with the deep scars of your own*
*childhood?*
*about angel choruses of peace on earth when you*
*are haunted by headlines on rising military*
*expenditures?*
*about preacher-talk of "goodwill on earth" when*
*you have just lost your job?*

What is there to celebrate? Maybe nothing—if the spirit of celebration is reserved only for the lighthearted and the lucky. But let us ponder another story, related by Clarence Forsberg. One day he visited a little chapel out in the Pacific Northwest. It was a frame church and had stained glass windows and a beautiful altar. As he left the church, he stopped to sign the guest register. Leafing through the pages to see if he recognized any of the names, he spied one particular entry. No name was listed, just the date and these words, "Thank you for a place to cry."

Could it be that in a world of tears having a place to cry is something to celebrate—especially when that place celebrates Christmas, and what Christmas celebrates is a heritage not of undiluted happiness but of indomitable hope?

—Melvin E. Wheatley, Jr.
*Christmas Is for Celebrating*

# A Litany for the Family

*Light the first purple candle; read Micah 7:7.*

**Leader:** "I wait in hope for God, my savior." That's what the prophet Micah said. This is the time of year that we remember the hope the birth of Jesus brought to the world. We share that same hope each year when we wait for Jesus' birth.

**All:** Our hopes are many.
We hope for peace, for love among all peoples.
We hope that everyone can have something to eat and a place to live.
We hope that businesses care about how they affect the world around them.
We hope that governments begin to understand each other.

**Leader:** All of that seems impossible.

**All:** Yes, it does. But not if we take one small thing at a time. We know that God works through us to bring about the kingdom Jesus talked about. We just have to let God do that!

**Prayer:** God of hopeful times, then, our prayer is this: Work through us to help make your world a better place for everyone. Amen.

**Family Activity:** If you don't have a family altar already, make one for Advent. You could use a card table or some other small table. You might want to set your nativity scene or Advent wreath there. You may want to write the verse from Micah 7:7 and place it above your altar.
Remember to place your wise men far away from your nativity scene. They have a long way to travel.

## Second Sunday in Advent

*Light the first and second purple candles; read Luke 3:1–6.*

**Leader:** "Get Ready!" "Get Ready!" That's what John the Baptist shouted to everyone who would listen.
**All:** Get ready for what?

**Leader:** Make the road ready for God's Son, who again brings with him the promise of a new time.

**All:** A time of no more hurting, no more fighting, no more greed.

**Leader:** So get ready, world!

**All:** Yes, and get ready schools and churches and families and neighborhoods. All of us—get ready! That means me, too!

**Prayer:** Dear God, we cannot bring the good news of your kingdom unless we understand what Jesus came to tell us. Help us open our minds and hearts so that we can begin to understand. Amen.

**Family Activity:** Everyone find a quiet, comfortable corner. Ask God to let you be a bringer of the good news. Sit quietly for five minutes. Then on a sheet of paper write or draw one way you might be a bringer of good news. Fold your paper and put it on your family altar. If you cannot think of anything, that's okay. Sometimes we have to be quiet a very long time. Move the wise men a little closer to the manger.

## Third Sunday in Advent

*Light the first two purple candles and either the pink or third purple candle—whichever your Advent set has; read Luke 1:46–55.*

**Leader:** "The time is coming!" said the prophet Zephaniah (chapter 3). He knew to expect great things.

**All:** And Mary in her beautiful song of praise knew to expect great things.

**Leader:** We know what Zephaniah and Mary knew. But sometimes we forget.

**All:** And when we forget, we are saying NO! to God—NO! to God's will for this beautiful world, NO! to God's gift of Jesus. We need to be YES! people.

**Prayer:** Dear God, when you sent Jesus to us—and each year when we remember your gift—you were saying YES! to us. Now help us say YES! to you. Amen.

**Family Activity:** Draw a big YES on a poster. Write some ways inside your letters that you can say YES to God's good news.
Move the wise men a little closer to the manger.

### Fourth Sunday in Advent

*Light the first three candles and the final purple candle; read Isaiah 61:1–4.*

**Leader:** The time is coming nearer—the time to welcome Jesus into our home once again.

**All:** We are excited; we can hardly wait; waiting has been so hard.

**Leader:** Have we made ourselves ready for Jesus to enter our lives again?

**All:** Yes!
We are watching; we are hoping. We are ready for God's peace and love. We are ready for God's gift.

**Prayer:** Dear God, you never give up on us. We have another chance to let your love grow even stronger in our hearts. Help us share your love with others. Amen.

**Family Activity:** Gather around your manger scene. If you have photographs of everyone in your family, set these photographs in the manger with the other figures. If you don't have a photograph, let each person draw a picture of herself or himself and put those pictures in the manger scene.
Move the wise men a little closer to the manger.

*Light the purple and pink candles. Read Luke 2:1–20. Now light the center candle—the white Christ candle—in your wreath.*

**Leader:** Tell all the people that their God has come.

**All:** Sing, heavens! Shout for joy, earth!

**Leader:** Tell all the people a child has been born!

**All:** And his name is Wonderful Counselor, Mighty God, Eternal Father, Prince of Peace. Hallelujah!

**Prayer:** Dear God, today we are very happy. Jesus has come again into our lives and our home. Thank you, God, for the best Christmas gift of all! Amen.

**Family Activity:** Have each person put something that for them means "happy" on the family altar. For instance, if Wendell were in your family, he would bring a carrot (or draw a carrot) to put on the family altar.

Move the wise men a little closer to the manger.

## Epiphany

*Before you begin, bring your wise men to the manger. Read Matthew 2:1–12*

**Leader:** On this day the wise men came from a far country to bring gifts to the Christ child. What gifts would we bring to the Christ child?

(Let each person write a note or draw a picture that represents a gift they would bring to the Christ child. Take your gifts and lay them beside the manger.)

**Leader:** "The light shines in darkness, and the darkness does not overcome it" (John 1:5).

**All:** The wise men followed a light, a star glowing brighter than any other.

**All:** And now it is time for us to follow a light—the light that Jesus brought into the world.

**All:** And it is time to spread that light to others—to our neighbors, to our friends, to those we study and work with.

**Leader:** Sometimes spreading that light may seem hard.

**All:** But Jesus will be with us as we spread God's good news of peace and love.

**Prayer:** Dear God, help us remember the wise men whenever we hesitate to share your news. Help us to understand that following a star may mean that we "return another way," as the wise men did, and that's okay. How could we behold the Christ child and be the same as we were? Amen.

*—Pockets* (staff)

# Something to Hope For

The old wicker rocking chair would squeak with a comforting rhythm as my grandmother held me on her lap, holding me close within her ample arms. As she rocked, the chair would travel along the wooden floor; and every so often she had to put me down, get up, and move it back to its starting place.

She would tell me tales of her youth and how she was married at thirteen in her bare feet. I would always beg her for one more story. But she would set me down from her lap and say, "Leave something to hope for, Child. It makes life sweet when times get hard."

Sometimes she would spellbind me by singing folk ditties filled with orphans lost in blizzards and sailors lost at sea. With my already vivid imagination captivated, I would beg her to sing just one more. Again, she would put me down and say, "Leave something to hope for, Child. It'll bring you dreams to keep you company."

One Mother's Day I scoured the whole neighborhood, picking every dandelion within a four-block square to make her a beautiful "bookay" tied with butcher's string. As she thanked me and solemnly placed them in her heirloom cut-glass vase, I got carried away and told her all of the wonderful things I was going to get her as soon as I grew up. She laughed that deep and hearty laugh of hers. Then she picked me up, carried me to the wicker chair, and began our afternoon ritual. "Mercy, Child," she said. "Leave me something to hope for. If I had all them things, I'd have nothing left to dream about, and life wouldn't be much to look forward to."

I do not know what became of the old rocker, but I now put my own child's dandelions in the cut-glass vase. And every now and then I remember her words. When times are hard, I always have something held in reserve to hope for.

When my dreams do not seem to be turning out the way I had expected, I can always move in another direction, undergirded with hope. I can smile and say, "Leave something to hope for, Child. It makes life sweet."

—**Marie Livingston Roy**
*alive now!*

# Our Responsibility in God's Creation

Read Isaiah 42:1–4;

1 Corinthians 13: 11–12.

Christianity has been accused of promising "pie in the sky by and by," while deferring action for social change in the present. But, as liberation theologians stress, since the Christian task is to transform society rather than merely to describe it, indifference in the presence of social injustice is unacceptable.

There has to be a continuing struggle to achieve a kind of society God intends for us all. "Thy will be done, on earth as in heaven," we pray. This is Christian hope that motivates us in the struggle for social transformation.

Christian hope is a compelling and necessary force, both for us personally as well as for the society at large. More than we realize, what we do now is determined by what we expect of the future. By the very nature of our personality we were created by our Maker to hope. A college student would not care to study if there were no hope of any reward after graduation. This reward could be tangible or intangible, visible or invisible—it doesn't matter. The end result, however, must be worthwhile. Otherwise, there would be no reason to work and struggle.

Hope of life in Christ and in his kingdom to an unimaginable degree is enough to motivate us, so that no obstacle can deter us in pursuit of the way, the truth, and the life.

*Prayer:* Lord, you have promised us a glorious future in Christ. Grant that among many changes of the world, we may continue to hope for what you have promised. Amen.

—S. Michael Yasutake
*The Upper Room Disciplines 1986*

# Will a Sign Come?

What's left of hope?
   A shattered, tattered world
   alternates between its cries of pain
   and moments of numbed silence,
   waiting, waiting
   for some sign of hope.

Will a sign come?
Well, if we look to humankind
   waiting for hope in the new sanctuaries
   of humanity:
      temples of science
      nuclear silo-cathedrals of death
      consultation altar-couches
         where men and women
         offer human sacrifice,
   we're doomed to disappointment and despair.

But there is more—
   A frail thin thread of light
   burst into the fullness of a star
   and hovers where a baby comes to birth,
   and in the infant's advent
   is our sign of hope.

               —Robin E. Van Cleef
               *alive now!*

# Sighted

Once we ate darkness
and ran shame-wild from the face
and rhetoric.
But now
the Christ, sweet Jesus,
is our hope.
Master of all,
come.

> —Evangeline Bri Abanes
> *alive now!*

# Mystery

It's a mystery, Lord,
in the midst
of a season of mysteries
defying reason:
   How could God be human
   or bread be flesh
   or wine, blood?
When I am tempted thus
to fantastic flights
of theological speculation,
remind me, Lord,
through human things
like straw and swaddling cloths,
that incarnation comes
and God shows divine life
through human lives—
   like mine.

        —Robin E. Van Cleef
        *alive now!*

# This Vining Wreath

Thanksgiving has never seemed real at our house. Last spring we had Easter and it was real, as if all of history and all of nature had agreed to do the thing in unison. Since then we have partitioned our time with Independence Day and Labor Day, Halloween and Thanksgiving—pleasant interruptions, long on food and drink but short on connectedness with humanity outside America.

But each year, almost before the last slice of mincemeat pie is gone, I can feel the activity accelerating—the real thing comes next! John wants to fetch the Advent wreath. Sam, Jr. wants the Advent calendar hung a week ahead of time. Rebecca wants to set the music out on the piano rack. The earth subtly joins in their agitation. The berries redden on the haw bushes. The holly grows thorny and turgid. The cold comes and the animals rest platonically close to each other.

The autumn is dying, as we all will die, and the days shorten into their ending. What and who will survive the cold and the dark will only be known four months hence when spring and the Easter light return. Whatever does survive will be changed, reshaped by the cold, reborn after deep sleep—acorn to sapling, larva to insect, God to flesh, time to forever.

It's coming, the mystery among us, and we begin the marking of most ancient time. The first Sunday of Advent, over the centuries, has come to honor Isaiah and his place as the first prophet to foretell the promise of an Incarnate Yahweh. Now all the earth once again awaits the coming of Christ.

—Phyllis A. Tickle
*What the Heart Already Knows*

# Mary to Elizabeth

This God our nation serves and worships is a God
Of dreams and most peculiar fantasies.
The old conceive, the untouched conceive,
And I think that henceforth we will not
Fix any tethers on the hands of God.
We will not say, "This cannot be," or murmur,
"Only a babbling fool believes such tales."
This God, this Holy One, startles me,
Bringing the impossible among us, making
A grand desire take shape as flesh and blood.
Who knows what may occur? If you and I
Have seen the truth indeed, known in ourselves
The ways of God, just think what deeds may shake
The world—the blind may one day see, the lame
May walk, the dead may live again, the sick
At heart may find new hope. Such shall we see.

—J. Stephen Lang
*alive now!*

# Can We Believe the Mystery?

When he did our flesh assure
That everlasting Man,
Mary held him in her womb
Whom heaven could not contain!
Who the mystery can believe!
Incomprehensible thou art;
Yet we still by faith conceive,
And bear thee in our heart.

—*Scripture Hymns* (1762)

"The Word became flesh and dwelt among us" (John 1:14, RSV). Who can explain God's assumption of human flesh in the form of Jesus? Who can explain Mary's conception of the Holy Child? These mysteries are unfathomable to the human mind. . . . We cannot subject the mystery to scientific analysis for verification. There are realities which transcend logic and science. We may say that we love someone and vow that such love is real, but we cannot prove it. Love transcends proof. We may produce what we view as tangible evidence of love, but the evidence is not the love itself. Love's reality resides within us. We can communicate that reality in our thoughts, words, actions, and emotions—in who we are. We personify love's reality.

The scripture tells us that "God is love" (1 John 4:8). In other words, God is best defined or described as Love, and Jesus personifies the reality of Love, Supreme Love, which goes in search of all human beings at all costs, even to death upon a cross. Jesus is the evidence that Love is real. Through the indwelling Spirit of Jesus, Love's reality resides within us. And though we do not fully comprehend it,

Yet we still by faith conceive
And bear thee in our heart.

—S T Kimbrough, Jr.
*Lost in Wonder*

# Advent

Here in the north,
barren cold, dry earth
and early dark

speak of greater dearth
and ultimate darkness.
What do we hope for?

What do we get?
A mystery: God in flesh.

I spend December

flexing my fingers
to seize the hem of
cloth that wrapped him.

Slippery as silk,
the coarse reality
of incarnation.

—Ellen Roberts Young
alive now!

# Like One More Chore

Like one more chore or Christmas tree display
I schedule you into my rushing life;
An hour on Sunday, if no friends or strife
Should interrupt; no ice or snow delay
The quick momentum of my busy day.
With children taking lessons, and the wife
Involved in charities, one has to knife
One's little pleasures in between the play
Of need and duty. Oh, your kind eyes chill,
When for a moment by the village crèche
I pause and song unravels through the night.
Of course, it's not a thing of time, but will;
And all the right priorities must mesh
For those who seek the healing of your light.

—Charles A. Waugaman
*alive now!*

# The One Thing Necessary

*Read 1 John 4:7–21*

The justice and peace that God revealed and established in Jesus stand midway between now and the time or state of fulfillment. They are "metaphorical." The justice of God is richer than what we can measure out onto the two pans of a legal dispute. The peace of God includes rest for the soul and satisfaction for hearts that have here no lasting city. So, like Jesus himself, these and other notions central to Christian life connote as much as they denote. Like Jesus himself, they are icons or sacraments that point the way to the mysterious simplicity of God. The one thing necessary in the spiritual life is that we keep opening ourselves to this mysterious simplicity. The only mortal failing is to close our souls and refuse to keep trying to hear what the Spirit is saying....

Jesus is for Christians the sacrament of human beings' encounter with the divine mystery. His life and person have clarified what everyone born of woman is about. He has overturned the flat, simplistic sense of "life" and "death," as Socrates also did. After Jesus, we have to estimate the success or failure of any person's life in more than worldly terms. The person rich in worldly accomplishments may be poor in wisdom and charity. The person considered of little account in the world may stand great in the eyes of God. Indeed, even this first bit of paradox has to be questioned, for further reflection makes us realize that poverty can twist people's spirits as well as their bodies. Good fortune can make people humble with gratitude. The more we ponder the one thing necessary, the more we realize that judgment, like vengeance, belongs to God alone.

If we push ourselves to stay open to the divine mystery and make its love our great treasure, we move outside the realm of any Caesar and attain at least the outskirts of God's rest.... More and more, I have come to think, serious spirituality walks the path of increasing surrender. John the Baptist caught much of this spirit when he gladly proclaimed that he had to decrease and Christ increase. In psychological terms, maturity means less egocentricity and self-concern. In philosophical terms, it means more objectivity. This objectivity is not unfeeling or impersonal. It takes away none of the wit and sparkle that we rightly love and find individualizing. Rather it makes us free like the dancer and the musician, who lose themselves in the objective reality of the music. Like the creative scientist, we should stand rapt before the complexities and beauties of a reality that colors us tiny. Like the Pauline mystic, we should live not for ourselves but for the Christ living in us. . . .

At home, at work, at church, our first job is to be a helper rather than a hinderer, a modest worker rather than a touchy supervisor. We may gradually become convinced that great changes in the current ways of doing business are necessary and so find ourselves revolutionaries of a sort. We may study the headline, watch the news, and gradually come to think that we have to say no to the people and policies ruling our land. But even in these cases our Johannine posture should continue. Thus we will think it no big deal to change to another branch of the church universal or join a file of antiwar protestors. Such a move will not be a display of ego or a cry for attention. It will be but the next step in our daily effort to go forward a bit further into the mystery and apparent purposes of God. . . .

The one thing necessary can animate many different styles and conceptual systems. What it can never do is make people hateful or despairing. Love of the genuine, truly mysterious God always tells us that there are more things in God's power than our tiny list of certainties ever dreamed. Similarly, the charity that really counts always tells us to keep trying, even when this is in the mode of a counsel to let go and take what comes. The peace that surpasses understanding, like the justice that this world never gives, only comes into sight when we have surrendered ourselves enough to let God truly reign. The political life necessitated by the gospel is but the other side of the gospel's call to prayer. When we gaze at our suffering neighbors unblinkingly, we know that only God can change things to the depth they require. When we slip below words and desires and self-concerns, it becomes obvious that we have to try to love our neighbors as ourselves. This love is the alpha and omega. This love is what will prevail when God is all in all.

*Can one be significantly human without loving the mystery of God?*

*Is humility a trustworthy sign of religious maturity?*

*What political convictions does the peace of Christ tend to foster?*

—John Carmody
*The Quiet Imperative*

# Between December And December

Between December
and December
we lose our way
sometimes.
Detours and
roads not taken
tantalize for sure.
A star appears,
a lure
toward truth
we can hold fast,
legacy from every
Christmas past.
Doors which were
never locked
are open
　　starshine is real
　　at mystery we kneel.

—Sharon Blessum
*alive now!*

# For a Sunday in Advent

I remember the blue-cold child
  who came to a winter world, O God,
    wherein those who were warm and well-fed
  knew not of his coming.
I know that for many people
  our world is a winter world.
There are the starving and the wandering,
    the victims of famine and of war.
There are in our nation
  those who face the debilitating fear of unemployment
    and the terrible frustration of not being needed or
    wanted.
And the blue-cold child will come again on Christmas Day.
In my remembering him,
  Let me not forget them,
    the helpless and the hungry,
  those who either have no songs to sing
    or no strength for singing.
For in my remembering him, O Lord,
  I become aware that he was a hand reaching out
    to the whole world,
  he was a gift to all humanity.


He was the warm fire of your love in a winter world.
He was your arm reached out to embrace the lost and the
      lonely,
    the lovable and the unlovable.
And in remembering him,
  I recall my own identity as one who has taken his hand,
    warmed my heart at the fire of your love,
    entered the embrace of your concern.
I am grateful.
And then in your presence, O God,
  I ask myself if my gratitude spills over into other lives.
I must confess I am not sure it does,
  at least not very often.

So I pray this Advent that my remembering may become
        renewal,
    my recollection enlargement.

Go with me as I move through these December days
    toward the Christmas morning
        where again the blue-cold child will cry under the
        winter sky.
    I remember Jesus, O God,
    and in the memory is the mystery of love,
        your love and our love,
    all love divine and human.
And the mystery is the memory of life
    in Jesus Christ our Lord. *Amen.*

—Kenneth G. Phifer
*A Book of Uncommon Prayer*

# Then and Now...With Healing in His Wings

"Then" means once upon a wonder
when old man Harold Quincy lived next door.
Old and "weird"—or so my sister said,
who knew somewhat of life;
she was nine years wise.

I was four and feared the Quincy place,
where, it was said, Harold spent his time
talking to his chickens.
Backyard bantams, mostly,
a few Rhode Island Reds,
which scratched and scavenged, clucking now and then,
to keep their chicks in tow. I stayed away,
but sometimes heard him mumbling through the hedge.
And once or twice I peeped
and saw the battered hat he wore
and noticed rusty stains in his mustache.
"Oh. That," my mother said and sniffed.
"Tobacco juice. He chews."
And so I peeped some more.
To watch him spit.
He did, though mostly what he did
was talk. And not just to the hens.
Sometimes I heard him talking...well...to God.
At least I thought so then. Who knows?
Perhaps his "Precious Lord's" were something else
   instead,
and on his cheeks the tears I thought were tears
were not.

But anyway, I wondered.
And then when Christmas came that year,
I wondered when we sang that song in church.

You know, the one where Harold's angels
sing "Glory" to the newborn king.
The king, I thought, was Jesus.
God's son. And Mary's.
Her father owned a donkey,
    and looked after the sheep,
    and was under the haystack, fast asleep,
    one cold winter's night that was so deep,
    when the angels' singing woke him up.
Harold's angels, wings feathered like his hens.
A wonder!

But, as my daughter likes to tell me,
in her nine-years world-wise voice,
"That was then, Dad, then.
This is *now*!" And I know she is right.
Now it is indeed. And what a now it is,
this now where
    mega weapons loom,
    new virus plagues alarm,
    the poorest poor still die.

In such a now the best of all good news
is still the tale, time-tattered,
of holiness enfleshed.
Into this, our now, he comes.
He comes. No less a wonder Now than Then.
He comes...
this man who calls himself a mother hen
and tucks the lost, chilled chicks into a feathered
    nest.
He comes...to us,
with Harold's angels' healing in his wings.

—Kenneth L. Gibble
*alive now!*

# The Singing of Angels

There must be always remaining
in everyone's life
some place for the singing of angels—
some place for that which in itself is breathlessly beautiful
and by an inherent prerogative
throwing all the rest of life
into new and created relatedness.
Something that gathers up in itself
all the freshets of experience
from the drab and commonplace areas of living
and glows in one bright white light of penetrating beauty and
    meaning—
then passes.
The commonplace is shot through now with new glory—
old burdens become lighter,
deep and ancient wounds lose much of their old, old hurting.
A crown is placed over our heads
that for the rest of our lives
we are trying to grow tall enough to wear.
Despite all of the crassness of life,
despite all the hardness of life,
despite all the harsh discords of life,
    life is saved by the singing of angels.

—Howard Thurman
*alive now!*

# A Deed of Love

Read Matthew 25:31–40

The King will answer them, "Truly, I say to you, as you did it to one of the least of these my brethren, you did it to me."
—Matthew 25:40 (RSV)

On a hillside on the outskirts of Seoul there is a little village for tuberculosis patients. One hundred of them live in small shanties. They lead a miserable life, not because of their struggle against the disease but because of their isolation from family and society.

In the middle of the village is a small church. A dedicated young minister had been serving this parish for seven years. He had nursed the patients, provided them small jobs, secured them medicines, and even helped with their injections. It was not an easy life for the minister.

After seven years, there came a time when he had to leave for another church. The farewell service was held on Christmas Sunday. The minister said in his final words to the people, "I have worked for you all these years, but I am afraid I have not achieved much." Then an elder, speaking on behalf of the patients, responded, "Pastor, you may not have achieved visible results. But you have planted God's love and eternal hope in our hearts."

PRAYER: Thank you, Jesus, that you have planted love and hope among despairing and suffering people. May we all live in that love and hope. Amen.

THOUGHT FOR THE DAY

Christ calls us to bring healing and hope to those who suffer.

—Choon Kwan Un (Korea)
*The Upper Room*

# We Give Out Love in Boxes

We give out love in boxes
wrapped, tied, tagged.
But the first Christmas gift
was a love
that needed no adornment
or disguise;
a love
that wrapped itself
around our tired hearts forever.

—Kari Sharp Hill
*alive now!*

# A Place for Love

Little Jeremy asked to know why
the crèche was under the coffee table—
perhaps to protect it from wind and snow
or cacophony from our holiday babel.

I told him a cave was a likely place
for shelter and refuge from the cold
so the spot we chose was a grotto of grace.
Answer enough for a six-year-old.

It was also true they were safer there
from his and his cousins' pillow fights.
Yet I was glad he was ready to care
whether the crèche had its human rights.

And I think he was pleased to need to seek
for the manager himself and happy to find
where a visitor would need to peek
to see the infant and Mary kind

and the rest of the Bethlehem entourage,
for his eyes were glowing with Christmas joy
as he knelt way down to their camouflage
and offered his love to God's new boy.

—Thomas John Carlisle
*alive now!*

# Why the Candles, Jonathan?

## A Children's Story

It was three days before Christmas, and Jonathan was feeling rotten. He wanted so much for his family to do something together. Last Christmas, his mom had been in the hospital. Jonathan remembered how hard it had been. He had felt lonely and afraid at Christmas, a time when he usually felt happy. This year Mom was much better. He knew he should feel happy, but sometimes Jonathan felt afraid again, just like last year. When he had tried to tell everybody how he felt, nobody seemed to have time to listen.

But Jonathan had a plan. He hoped it would work. He checked the big brown bag to make sure he had everything: a package of popcorn, already popped; four packets of hot chocolate mix; cups and napkins; and four long red candles. Everything he needed for a great party—if only his family would come.

Jonathan hurried toward the kitchen. *Mom will love my surprise,* he thought. The smell of warm cinnamon cookies reached his nose. His mother smiled and handed Jonathan one to taste-test, then continued mixing butter and sugar in a big wooden bowl. Jonathan ate the cookie quickly, then waved the brown bag he was carrying and said, "Mom, I've got a surprise for the family. Come into the living room, and I'll show you. It's the *neatest* idea for Christmas."

"Jonathan, your timing is off," his mom said. "Right now I'm up to my elbows in flour, and the only thing I can think about is getting these cookies finished in time for the Christmas cookie exchange. We can talk later."

Joanathan was disappointed, but he tried to be cheerful. "Sure, Mom; I'll find Dad and tell him about it."

His mom smiled and handed him two more cookies. "One for Dad," she said.

Jonathan whistled as he headed for the living room, where

his dad was struggling to separate several strings of Christmas lights. As Jonathan walked in, his dad grinned and stopped for a moment to eat the cookie Jonathan handed him.

"Jonathan, could you grab this end and hang onto it for a minute? I'd like to put these up around the window, but they're all tangled together."

Jonathan took the string of lights. "Dad, I've got a great idea for..."

"Could you pull a little tighter on your end?" his father interrupted. "Sorry, Son. I don't have time to listen right now. If we're going to be ready for Christmas, I need to get these lights up tonight."

Jonathan sighed. "Sure, Dad." He straightened the string of lights, untangling knots as he went. The wind blowing outside made him feel sad.

Fifteen minutes later, Jonathan climbed the stairs to his brother Scott's room. Scott was almost twelve, three years older than Jonathan. If he liked Jonathan's party idea, the two of them could set it up and surprise Mom and Dad. Jonathan suddenly felt cheerful again. Scott was hunched over his desk as Jonathan walked in with the brown bag in his hand. He looked up briefly. "Hi, shrimp."

Jonathan felt dumb whenever Scott called him "shrimp" —like he was only in kindergarten or something instead of fourth grade. Scott was wrapping colored string around an orange juice can that was dripping with glue. "It's going to be a pencil holder for Dad for Christmas," he explained. "Pretty neat, huh?"

Jonathan wasn't sure this mess would ever look like a pencil holder, but he thought it best not to say anything about it. "Hey, Scott, I've got a neat idea, too. It's something the whole family can do together. Look!" He opened the bag and took out the candles.

Scott didn't even look up. "Oh, come on, Jonathan. You always have such weird ideas. Everybody's getting ready for Christmas. We don't have time for your dumb games."

Jonathan felt awful. He was afraid he might start to cry.

Scott would really tease him if he did that. Jonathan turned and headed for the door. Scott called after him. "Hey, Jonathan, I was just kidding. Want to help with the pencil holder? It can be from both of us."

But Jonathan knew those tears were ready to pop out any minute. He took his brown bag and headed back downstairs. By now, the wind was really whipping around the house. He could hear the big trees in the backyard creaking in the wind, and the sound made him feel nervous. He went into the living room and sat down by the fire. It was almost out because everyone was too busy to keep it going. That was the trouble. Everyone was too busy.

He watched out the front window for a few minutes. Now the snow was so thick that he could barely see the house across the street. The wind was blowing so hard that the little trees in the front yard were bent almost double. Just then, without any warning, all the lights in the house went out. All was silent. Even the wind was quiet for a moment. Suddenly, there were banging noises as Scott bumped into things on his way to the stairs. Jonathan's heart was pounding as he sat alone in the dark. He was glad to see the shadowy shapes of his mom and dad and Scott coming into the room. His dad sounded cross, "Don't we have any candles in this house? I can't see a thing."

Jonathan had a wonderful idea. "Sure, Dad. I have some right here. This is what I wanted to tell you about."

"About candles?" His dad sounded puzzled.

"The candles are part of it. It's a party, Dad. Just for our family. My teacher told us about it. He said it's a custom in some families. When we light the candles, we're supposed to think of one thing that we really like about the person sitting next to us and tell it to them."

Jonathan wasn't sure what to do next. He wanted so much for them to understand. He dug for the matches and lit one candle. Then he said, "I've got popcorn and hot chocolate mix, too. So it can be a real party."

For a few moments everyone was quiet. Jonathan wondered what they were thinking. They probably thought his idea was dumb. He wished he hadn't said anything.

Just then his father spoke. "That's a great idea, Son. I think maybe the rest of us have been missing the boat a little. Last year Mom was sick, and we couldn't have the kind of family Christmas that we wanted. This year we're together again, but we've all been rushing around doing things instead of making time for each other. Let's light some more of those candles."

Jonathan's mom moved closer and put her arm around him. Then Scott gave his shoulder a quick squeeze. Jonathan knew it meant "I'm sorry." Even before the candles were lit, Jonathan began to feel a glow. He didn't feel afraid any more. This was going to be a great Christmas!

—Peggy King Anderson
*Pockets*

# Spilling the Purse

Read Luke 23:39–47

Being in agony [Jesus] was praying very fervently; and His sweat became like drops of blood, falling down upon the ground. —Luke 22:44 (NASB)

My family and I were seated in a waiting room of the hospital, flanked by many friends who had come to offer their support. Our daughter, Melanie, had been seriously injured in an automobile accident just hours before, and we were all huddled together as her life hung in the balance. Melanie died, but God did not abandon us.

Among the many acts of love that overwhelmed us was one I will never forget. My friend Susan sat close by as I searched my bag for mints, chewing gum, anything at all that might make me feel just a little more comfortable. Realizing what I wanted, she searched nervously in her purse, then finally turned it upside down, offering me anything and everything that was inside.

As she lovingly spilled her purse, I thought of Jesus stretching out his arms and giving all he had—his very life—in love for us all.

*PRAYER:* O God of perfect love, as you emptied your life for us, make us willing to empty our hearts for one another. In Jesus' name. Amen.

THOUGHT FOR THE DAY

All of God's provision is poured out for us.

—Jan Carpenter (Minnesota)
*The Upper Room*

# Love in Action

Read 1 John 4:11–18

Dear children, let us not love with words or tongue but with actions and in truth.
—1 John 3:18 (NIV)

The day before Christmas Eve was cold, wet, and rainy—dismal. That was an accurate description of my mood as well. What with all the hustle and bustle of the season, I felt physically and emotionally depleted.

Our dog Clementine, a German weimaraner, had her problems, too. She was old and had a bad case of pelvic arthritis, and the weather was to be unusually cold. My husband said, "We need to fix Clementine a warm place to lie down. The cold will cause her a lot of pain."

When we got Clementine's bed ready, we went out to find her. We were startled by what we saw. Overhearing what his daddy had said, our six-year-old son had gone outside, found Clementine, and wrapped his body around her to keep her warm. He loves Clementine.

God used our son's loving act to remind me of the reason for celebrating Christmas. Jesus' coming to the world was God's loving response to our need. In turn, Jesus expects us to respond in love to those who need us.

*PRAYER:* Lord Jesus Christ, thank you for coming to us. Help me to share love with others, that they may understand your love for them. Amen.

THOUGHT FOR THE DAY

Love takes action to end suffering.

—Sandra Brooks (South Carolina)
*The Upper Room*

# *Four*

## Peace

*When he comes...,
people all over the earth
will acknowledge his
greatness,
and he will bring peace.*

Micah 5:4–5, TEV

# The Peace Lamb

Read Isaiah 9:2–7

His name shall be called...Prince of Peace.
—Isaiah 9:6 (KJV)

In one part of the range, a peaceful solution was discovered in the war between the ranchers who raised cattle and those who raised sheep. Each group feared the other. One sheep owner carried an orphan lamb, of which there were many each spring, to a neighbor cattle rancher, saying, "I've got so many orphan lambs I can't raise them all. Will you help? If you would raise this lamb on a bottle, it would really be a favor." He made similiar requests of other neighbors.

The ranchers could not resist the charm of the growing lambs, and they soon came to know that the sheep owners could be trusted. Finally peace came. The peace lambs made the difference.

Doesn't that make the gospel understandable in our day? God sent Jesus, a peace child, that we humans might learn to trust God. God sent a peace lamb who would become the Prince of Peace, that we might hear and understand the better way and walk in the light of God's love.

*PRAYER:* O God, silently now we open our hearts to your presence, which is our hope. We thank you for your presence among us—as a peace child, as light, as love. Amen.

## Thought for the Day

The Christmas season is a time for us to express our gratitude for God's gift to us in Jesus.

—Orval H. Austin (New Mexico)
*The Upper Room*

# A Prayer for Peace

I need your peace, O God,
Not so much peace from the strife in the world—
I have a way of turning off my hearing
when it comes to the suffering of humanity.
Miners strike, and I retire to my book;
Hostages suffer, and I think, interesting;
Children are hungry, but I can do nothing about it.
Don't tell me; I don't want to hear.
I don't need peace from the troubles of the world.
If anything, I need to be disturbed even more.

I don't need peace in my more private world.
I have learned how to overlook the irritating habits
of those who are close to me.
I can ignore the people whose attitudes differ from
    my own.
Peace is not difficult to achieve
when those around me just don't matter.
It is good for me to discover they *do* matter.
I grow when I have to pay attention,
and respect the differences I discover
in those around me.

The peace I need is an inward thing.
Peace from the noisy strife of my troubled soul.
Listen, God, and you will hear
pride arguing with guilt,
hurt feelings moaning about their lovelessness,
while selfishness bullies all others away.
Self-doubt nags at self-confidence
while self-centeredness tyrannizes all.

Yes, Lord, I need your peace;
but I need it within me.
Still the clamoring voices

and tune my ear to hear
your still, small voice
that speaks to me of better things—
of the light that comes from your will,
the strength that lives in your hand.
Give me your peace, O Lord,
that I may live your peace
in a strife-torn world.
Amen.

—George L. Miller
*alive now!*

# The Peace between Us

The theme of peace . . . points to the center of the gospel of Jesus Christ, which Paul expressed with typical directness: "He is the peace between us" (Eph. 2:14, JB). Paul perceived that Christ's death on the cross had inaugurated the reign of God's peace for which Israel had waited so long. The spell of religious and political antagonism that divided the world between Jews and Gentiles had been broken. In its place, embodied in Jesus Christ and visible in those who gathered in his name, was a new humanity united in community and reconciled with God. For this reason, Paul was convinced that practicing the art of peace was essential to the meaning of the church: "May the peace of Christ reign in your hearts, because it is for this that you were called together as parts of one body" (Col. 3:15, —JB). . . .

When strangers greet one another in the name of Jesus, when enemies embrace because of Jesus, when congregations seek truth in remembrance of Jesus, then the peace of Christ is reigning in human hearts. Diversity then ceases to divide and instead begins to enrich a deeper unity in Jesus Christ. So fundamental and comprehensive is this unity that Paul could say: "There is neither Jew nor Greek, there is neither slave nor free, there is neither male nor female; for you are all one in Christ" (Gal. 3:28, RSV).

—John S. Mogabgab
*Weavings*

# The Peace That Is Not of This World

*Peace I bequeath to you, my own peace I give you, a peace the world cannot give, this is my gift to you.*
—John 14:27 (JB)

During the past two years I moved from Harvard to Daybreak, that is, from an institution for the best and brightest to a community for mentally handicapped people. Daybreak, close to Toronto, is part of an international federation of communities called l'Arche—the Ark—where mentally handicapped men and women and their assistants try to live together in the spirit of the Beatitudes. I live in a house with six handicapped people and four assistants. None of the assistants is specially trained to work with people with mental handicaps, but we receive all the help we need from doctors, psychiatrists, behavioral management people, social workers, and physiotherapists in town. When there are no special crises we live together as a family, gradually forgetting who is handicapped and who is not. We are simply John, Bill, Trevor, Raymond, Adam, Rose, Steve, Jane, Naomi, and Henri. We all have our gifts, our struggles, our strengths and weaknesses. We eat together, play together, pray together, and go out together. We all have our own preferences in terms of work, food, and movies, and we all have our problems in getting along with someone in the house, whether handicapped or not. We laugh a lot. We cry a lot, too. Sometimes both at the same time. Every morning when I say, "Good morning, Raymond," he says, "I am not awake yet. Saying good morning to everyone each day is unreal." Christmas Eve Trevor wrapped marshmallows in silver paper as peace gifts for everyone, and at the Christmas dinner he climbed on a chair, lifted his glass, and said, "Ladies and gentlemen, this is not a celebration, this is Christmas." When one of the men speaking on the phone with someone was bothered by the cigarette smoke of an assistant, he yelled angrily "Stop smoking; I can't hear." And every guest who comes for dinner is received by Bill with the question, "Hey, tell me, what is a turkey in suspense?" When the newcomer confesses ignorance, Bill, with a big grin on his face, says, "I will tell you tomorrow." And then he starts laughing so loud that the visitor has to laugh with him whether he finds the joke funny or not so funny.

That is l'Arche; that is Daybreak; that is the family of ten I am living with day in and day out. What can life in this family of a few poor people reveal about the peace of Christ for which we are searching? Let me tell you the story of Adam, one of the ten people in our home, and let him become the silent spokesman for the peace that is not of this world.

Never having worked with handicapped people, I was not only apprehensive but even afraid to enter this unfamiliar world. This fear did not lessen when I was invited to work directly with Adam. Adam is the weakest person of our family. He is a twenty-five-year-old man who cannot speak, cannot dress or undress himself, cannot walk alone or eat without much help. He does not cry, or laugh, and only occasionally makes eye contact. His back is distorted and his arm and leg movements are very twisted. He suffers from severe epilepsy and, notwithstanding heavy medication, there are few days without grand-mal seizures. Sometimes, as he grows suddenly rigid, he utters a howling groan, and on a few occasions I have seen a big tear coming down his cheek. It takes me about an hour and a half to wake Adam up, give him his medication, undress him, carry him into his bath, wash him, shave him, clean his teeth, dress him, walk him to the kitchen, give him his breakfast, put him in his wheelchair, and bring him to the place where he spends most of the day with different therapeutic exercises. When a grand-mal seizure occurs during this sequence of activities, much more time is needed, and often he has to return to sleep to regain some of the energy spent during such a seizure.

I tell you all of this not to give you a nursing report but to share with you something quite intimate. After a month of working this way with Adam, something started to happen to me that never had happened to me before. This deeply handicapped young man, who by many outsiders is considered a vegetable, a distortion of humanity, a useless animal-like creature who should not have been allowed to be born, started to become my dearest companion. As my fears gradually decreased, a love started to emerge in me so full of tenderness and affection that most of my other tasks seemed boring and superficial compared with the hours spent with Adam. Out of this broken body and broken mind emerged a most beautiful human being offering me a greater gift than I would ever be able to offer him.

It is hard for me to find adequate words for this experience, but somehow Adam revealed to me who he was and who I was and how we could love each other. As I carried his naked body into the water, made big waves to let the water run fast around his chest and neck, rubbed noses with him, and told him all sorts of stories about him and me, I knew that two friends were communicating far beyond the realm of thought or emotion. Deep speaks to deep, spirit speaks to spirit, heart speaks to heart. I started to realize that there was a mutuality of love not based on shared knowledge or shared feelings, but on shared humanity. The longer I stayed with Adam, the more clearly I started to see him as my gentle teacher, teaching me what no book, school, or professor ever could have taught me.

Am I romanticizing, making something beautiful out of something ugly, projecting my hidden need to be a father on this deeply retarded man, spiritualizing what in essence is a shameful human condition that needs to be prevented at all costs? I am enough of a psychologically trained intellectual to raise these questions. Recently, as I was writing this article, Adam's parents came for a visit. I asked them, "Tell me, during all the years you had Adam in your home, what did he give you?" His father smiled and said without a moment of hesitation, "He brought us peace...his is our peacemaker...our son of peace."

Let me, then, tell you about Adam's peace, a peace which the world cannot give. I am moved by the simple fact that probably the most important task I have is to give words to the peace of one who has no words. The gift of peace hidden in Adam's utter weakness is a gift not of the world but certainly a gift *for* the world. For this gift to become known, someone has to lift it up and hand it on. That maybe is the deepest meaning of being an assistant to handicapped people. It is helping them to share their gifts.

Adam's peace is first of all a peace rooted in *being*. How simple a truth, but how hard to live! Being is more important than doing. Adam can do nothing. He is completely dependent on others every moment of his life. His gift is his pure *being with us*. Every time in the evening when I run home to "do" Adam—that means help him with his supper and put him to bed—I realize that the best thing I can do for Adam is to be with him. If Adam wants anything, it is that you be with him. And indeed that is the great joy: paying total attention to his breathing, his eating, his careful steps; looking at how he tries to lift a spoon to his mouth, or offers his left arm a little to make it easier for you to take off his shirt; always wondering about possible pains that he cannot express but that still ask for relief.

Most of my past life has been built around the idea that my value depends on what I do. I made it through grade school, high school, and university. I earned my degrees and awards and I made my career. Yes, with many others, I fought my way up to the lonely top of a little success, a little popularity, and a little power. But as I sit beside the slow and heavy-breathing Adam, I start seeing how violent that journey was. So filled with desires to be better than others, so marked by rivalry and competition, so pervaded with compulsions and obsessions and so spotted with moments of suspicion, jealousy, resentment, and revenge. Oh sure, most of what I did was called ministry, the ministry of justice and peace, the ministry of forgiveness and reconciliation, the ministry of healing and wholeness. But when those who want peace are as interested in success, popularity, and power as those who want war, what then *is* the real difference between war and peace? When the peace is as much of this world as the war, what other choice is there but the choice between a war which we euphemistically call pacification and a peace in which the peacemakers violate each others' deepest values?

Adam says to me, "Peace is first of all the art of being." I know he is right because after four months of being with Adam I am discovering in myself an inner at-homeness that I did not know before. I am even feeling the unusual desire to do a lot less and be a lot more, preferably with Adam.

As I cover him with his sheets and blankets and turn out the lights, I pray with Adam. He is always very quiet as if he knows that my praying voice sounds a little different from my speaking voice. I whisper in his ear, "May all the angels protect you," and often he looks up to me from his pillow and seems to know what I am talking about. Since I began to pray with Adam, I have come to know better than before that praying is being with Jesus and simply wasting time with him. Adam keeps teaching me that.

Adam's peace is not only a peace rooted in being but also a peace rooted in the heart. That true peace belongs to the heart is such a radical statement that only people as handicapped as Adam seem to be able to get it across! Somehow during the centuries we have come to believe that what makes us human is our mind. Many people who do not know any Latin still seem to know the definition of a human being as a reasoning animal: *rationale animal est homo* (Seneca). But Adam keeps telling me over and over again that what makes us human is not our mind but our heart, not our ability to think but our ability to love. Whoever speaks about Adam as a vegetable or an animal-like creature misses the sacred mystery that Adam is fully capable of receiving and giving love. He is fully human, not a little bit human, not half human, not nearly human, but fully, completely human because he is all heart. And it is our heart that is made in the image and likeness of God. If this were not the case, how could I ever say to you that Adam and I love each other? How could I ever experience new life from simply being with him? How could I ever believe that moving away from teaching many men and women to being taught by Adam is a real step forward? I am speaking here about something very, very real. It is the primacy of the heart.

Let me quickly say here that by heart I do not mean the

seat of human emotions in contrast to the mind as the seat of human thought. No, by heart I mean the center of our being where God has hidden the divine gifts of trust, hope, and love. The mind tries to understand, grasp problems, discern different aspects of reality, and probe the mysteries of life. The heart allows us to enter into relationships and become sons and daughters of God and brothers and sisters of each other. Long before our mind is able to exercise its power, our heart is already able to develop a trusting human relationship. I am convinced that this trusting human relationship even precedes the moment of our birth.

Here we are touching the origin of the spiritual life. Often people think that the spiritual life is the latest in coming and follows the development of the biological, emotional, and intellectual life. But living with Adam and reflecting on my experience with him makes me realize that God's loving Spirit has touched us long before we can walk, feel, or talk. The spiritual life is given to us from the moment of our conception. It is the divine gift of love that makes the human person able to reveal a presence much greater than him or herself. When I say that I believe deeply that Adam can give and receive love and that there is a true mutuality between us, I do not make a naive psychological statment overlooking his severe handicaps. I am speaking about a love between us that transcends all thoughts and feelings, precisely because it is rooted in God's love, a love that precedes all human loves. The mystery of Adam is that in his deep mental and emotional brokenness he has become so empty of all human pride that he has become the preferable mediator of that first love. Maybe this will help you see why Adam is giving me a whole new understanding of god's love for the poor and the oppressed. He has offered me a new perspective on the well-known "preferential option" for the poor.

The peace that flows from Adam's broken heart is not of this world. It is not the result of political analysis, round table debates, discernment of the signs of the times, or well-thought-out strategies. All these activities of the mind have their role to play in the complex process of peacemaking. But they all will become easily perverted to a new way of warmaking if they are not put into the service of the divine peace that flows from the broken heart of those who are called the poor in spirit.

The third and most tangible quality of Adam's peace is that, while rooted more in being than in doing and more in the heart than the mind, it is a peace that always calls forth community. The most impressive aspect of my life at l'Arche is that the handicapped people hold us together as a family and that the most handicapped people are the true center of gravity of our togetherness. Adam in his total vulnerability calls us together as a family. And in fact, from the perspective of community formation, he turns everything upside down. The weakest members are the assistants. We come from different countries—Brazil, the United States, Canada, and Holland—and our commitments are ambiguous at best. Some stay longer than others, but most move on after one or two years. Closer to the center are Raymond, Bill, John, and Trevor, who are relatively independent, but still need much help and attention. They are permanent members of the family. They are with us for life, and they keep us honest. Because of them, conflicts never last very long, tensions are talked out, and disagreements resolved. But at the heart of our community are Rose and Adam, both deeply handicapped. And the weaker of the two is Adam.

Adam is the most broken of us all, but without any doubt the strongest bond among us all. Because of Adam there is always someone home, because of Adam there is a quiet rhythm in the house, because of Adam there are moments of silence, because of Adam there are always words of affection, gentleness, and tenderness, because of Adam there is patience and endurance, because of Adam there are smiles and tears visible to all, because of Adam there is always space for mutual forgiveness and healing...yes, because of Adam there is peace among us. How otherwise could people from such different nationalties and cultures, people with such different characters and with such an odd variety of handicaps, whether mental or not, live together in peace? Adam truly calls us together around him and molds this motley group of strangers into a family. Adam, the weakest among us, is our true peacemaker. How mysterious are God's ways: "God chose those who by human standards are fools, to shame the wise; he chose those who by human standards are weak to shame the strong, those who by human standards are common and contemptible—indeed who count for nothing—to reduce to nothing all those who do count for something, so that no human being might feel boastful before God" (I Cor. 1:27–30 *author paraphrase*). Adam gives flesh to these words of Paul. He teaches me the true mystery of community.

Most of my adult life I have tried to show the world that I could do it on my own, that I needed others only to get me back on my lonely road. Those who helped me have helped me to become a strong, independent, self-motivated, creative man who would be able to survive in the long search for individual freedom. With many others, I wanted to become a self-sufficient star. And most of my fellow intellectuals joined me in that desire. But all of us highly trained individuals are facing today a world on the brink of total destruction. And now we start to wonder how we might join forces to make peace! What kind of peace can this possibly be? Who can paint a portrait of people who all want to take the center seat? Who can build a beautiful church with people who are only interested in erecting the tower? Who can bake a birthday cake with people who only want to put the candles on? You all know the problem. When all want the honor of being the final peacemaker, there never will be peace.

Adam needs many people and nobody can boast about anything. Adam will never be better. His constant seizures even make it likely that medically things will only get worse. There are no successes to claim, and everyone who works with him only does a little bit. My part in his life is very, very small. Some cook for him, others do his laundry, some give him massages, others play him music, take him for a walk, a swim, or a ride. Some look after his blood pressure and regulate his medicine, others look after his teeth. But though with all this assistance Adam does not change and often seems to slip away in a state of total exhaustion, a community of peace has emerged around him. It is a community that certainly does not want to put its light under a basket, because the peace community that Adam has called forth is not there just for Adam, but for all who belong to Adam's race. It is a community that proclaims that God has chosen to descend among us in complete weakness and vulnerability and thus to reveal to us the glory of God.

Thus, as you see, Adam is gradually teaching me something about the peace that is not of this world. It is a peace not constructed by tough competition, hard thinking, and individual stardom, but rooted in simply being present to each other, a peace that speaks about the first love of God by which we are all held and a peace that keeps calling us to community, a fellowship of the weak. Adam has never said a word to me. He will never do so. But every night as I put him to bed I say "thank you" to him. How much closer can one come to the Word that became flesh and dwells among us?

I have told you about Adam and about Adam's peace. But you are not part of l'Arche, you do not live at Daybreak, you are not a member of Adam's family. Like me, however, you search for peace and want to find peace in your heart, your family, and your world. But looking around us in the world we see concentration camps and refugee camps; we see overcrowded prisons; we see the burning of villages, genocidal actions, kidnappings, torture, and murder; we see starving children, neglected elderly, and countless men and women without food, shelter, or a job. We see people sleeping in the city streets, young boys and girls selling themselves for others' pleasure; we see violence and rape and the desperation of millions of fearful and lonely people. Seeing all this, we realize that there is no peace in our world. And still...that is what our hearts desire most. You and I may have tried giving money, demonstrating, overseas projects, and many other things, but as we grow older we are faced with the fact that the peace we waited for still has not come. Something in us is in danger of growing cold, bitter, and resentful, and we are tempted to withdraw from it all and limit ourselves to the easier task of personal survival. But that is a demonic temptation.

I have told you about Adam and his peace to offer you a quiet guide with a gentle heart who gives you a little light to walk with through this dark world. Adam does not solve anything. Even with all the support he receives, he cannot change his own utter poverty. As he grows older, he grows poorer and poorer and poorer. A little infection, an unhappy fall, an accidental swallowing of his own tongue during a seizure, and any one of many other small incidents may take him suddenly away from us. When he dies, nobody will be able to boast about anything. And still, what a light he brings! In Adam's name I therefore say to you, "Do not give up working for peace. But always remember that the peace you are working for is not of this world. Do not let yourself be distracted by the great noises of war, the dramatic descriptions of misery, and the sensational expressions of human cruelty. The newspapers, movies, and war novels may make you numb, but they do not create in you a true desire for peace. They tend to create feelings of shame, guilt, and powerlessness and these feelings are the worst motives for peace work."

Keep your eyes on the Prince of Peace. He is the one who does not cling to his divine power; the one who refuses to turn stones into bread, jump from great heights, and rule with great power; the one who says, "Blessed are the poor, the gentle, those who mourn, and those who hunger and thirst for righteousness; blessed are the merciful, the pure in heart, the peacemakers and those who are persecuted in the cause of uprightness" (see Matt. 5:3–11); the one who touches the lame, the crippled and the blind; the one who speaks words of forgiveness and encouragement; the one who dies alone, rejected and despised. Keep your eyes on him who becomes poor with the poor, weak with the weak, and who is rejected with the rejected. He is the source of all peace.

Where is this peace to be found? The answer is clear. In weakness. First of all, in our own weakness, in those places of our heart where we feel most broken, most insecure, most in agony, most afraid. Why there? Because there our familiar ways of controlling our world are being stripped away; there we are called to let go of doing much, thinking much, and relying on our self-sufficiency. Right where we are weakest, the peace which is not of this world is hidden.

In Adam's name I say to you, "Claim that peace that remains unknown to so many and make it your own. Because with that peace in your heart you will have new eyes to see and new ears to hear and gradually recognize that same peace in places you would have least expected." Not long ago I was in Honduras. It was my first time in Central America since I had come to Daybreak and become friends with Adam. I suddenly reaized that I was a little less consumed by anger about the political manipulations, a little less distracted by the blatant injustices, and a little less paralyzed by the realization that the future of Honduras looks very dark. Visiting the severely handicapped Raphael in the l'Arche community near Tegucigalpa, I saw the same peace I had seen in Adam, and hearing many stories about the gifts of joy offered by the poorest of the poor to the oh-so-serious assistants who came from France, Belgium, the United States, and Canada, I knew that peace is the gift of God often hidden from the wise and wealthy and revealed to the inarticulate and poor.

I am not saying that the questions about peace in Central America, Afghanistan, Northern Ireland, South Africa, Iran, and Iraq are no longer important. Far from that, I am only saying that the seeds of national and international peace are already sown on the soil of our own suffering and the suffering of the poor, and that we truly can trust that these seeds, like the mustard seeds of the gospel, will produce large shrubs in which many birds can find a place to rest. As long as we think and live as if there is no peace yet and that it all is going to depend on ourselves to make it come about, we are on the road of self-destruction. But when we trust that the God of love has already given the peace we are searching for, we will see this peace breaking through the broken soil of our human condition and we will be able to let it grow fast and even heal the economic and political maladies of our time. With this trust in our hearts, we will be able to hear those words: "Blessed are the peacemakers, for they shall inherit the earth." It fills me with a special joy that all the Adams of this world will be the first to receive this inheritance.

Many people live in the night; a few live in the day. We all know about night and day, darkness and light. We know about it in our hearts; we know about it in our families and communities; we know about it in our world. The peace that the world does not give is the light that dispels the darkness. Every bit of that peace makes the day come!

Let me conclude with an old Hasidic tale that summarizes much of what I have tried to say.

A rabbi asked his students, "How can we determine the hour of dawn, when the night ends and the day begins?"

One of his students suggested, "When from a distance you can distinguish between a dog and a sheep?"

"No," was the answer from the rabbi.

"Is it when one man can distinguish between a fig tree and a grape vine?" asked a second student.

"No," the rabbi said.

"Please tell us the answer, then" said the students.

"It is, then," said the wise teacher, "when you can look into the face of human beings and you have enough light (in you) to recognize them as your brothers and sisters. Up until then it is night and darkness is still with us."

Let us pray for the light. It is the peace the world cannot give.

—Henri J.M. Nouwen
*Weavings*

# Unto Us a Child Is Born

ISAIAH 9:2–7

*Of the increase of his government and of peace*
*there will be no end,*
*upon the throne of David and over his kingdom,*
*to establish it, and to uphold it*
*with justice and with righteousness*
*from this time forth and for evermore.*
*The zeal of the Lord of hosts will do this.*
—Isaiah 9:7, RSV

The South African government, and those who support it, believe that apartheid is the best way of creating and maintaining peace. For over 333 years, when blacks of South Africa were quiet and reconciled to the oppressive system, it was considered that there was peace. And when, today, women sit in quiet desperation about equal rights with men, the male-dominated world thinks that there is peace. Whenever oppressed groups are quietly hurting under circumstances that would be intolerable to other people, then the establishment and its constituency think they have peace.

Is this peace? This kind of peace is like undetected cancer. The absence of a reaction to ill-treatment and injustice should never be regarded as peace, because it can only be peace *without* justice.

Isaish 9:2–7 deals primarily with a human condition infested with war and symbols of war. But there is a message of hope. A new king would overthrow the oppressor, dismantle the symbols of war, and establish an era of peace. Christians have adopted this message and have accepted Jesus as the One qualified to be mighty God and Prince of Peace.

Peace with justice is, therefore, possible on Jesus' terms only. True peace with justice can be ushered into our various habitats and circumstances only when we start with Jesus and take seriously the command, "You shall love your neighbor as yourself" (Matt. 22:39, RSV). We must learn to empathize daily with all people, realizing seriously and sincerely that God made all people of the world with one blood (Acts 17:26)—whether they are poor or rich, men or women, young or old, black, brown, yellow, red, or white. All are children of God who—especially today—hunger and thirst after peace with justice. All mothers, irrespective of social status, race, color, or creed suffer the same labor pain when they bring people of God into the world. These mothers feel the same pain and sorrow when their children are deprived of a peace with righteousness and justice.

On a personal level, peace with justice is tranquility and harmony of the soul. On a social level, peace with justice is the absence of humanly inflicted pain and the presence of an abundance of liberty based on love. The best way of creating and promoting peace is to truly and sincerely love people and to work hard to create a peace based on that love.

Let us ponder these questions honestly. How can we restore and maintain peace with justice in family, group, church, country, and the world? Have I been doing to and for others those things I wish people would do to and for me? How would I feel if my attitude and behavior toward others were directed toward me?

### Prayer

Lord Jesus, you are the only true Prince of Peace. Please forgive us our lack of justice in the things we do or do not do in the name of peace. Fill us now with your true peace, which surpasses all understanding; and help us to overthrow the power of evil and darkness from the throne of our hearts. Empower us so that we may be true messengers and instruments of peace with justice. And let it begin with me and in my home. May our world accept Jesus' terms of peace with justice. Amen.

—Abel T. Muzorewa
*Seasons of Peace*

# God of Compassionate Justice

God of compassionate justice,
  you have called us to do good,
  and we have asked, "But what is
  goodness?"

You have called us to love our
  neighbor, and still we debate the
  boundaries of our neighborhood.

You have called us to lay down
  our lives in service, and
  we have excused ourselves with
  explanations you wouldn't believe!

Renew your love in us, and
  help us live in simple obedience
  to your will.

In your will let us find and make
  peace.
  Amen.

—James E. Magaw
*alive now!*

# God's Peace

Read Philippians 4:10–13

God's peace, which is far beyond human understanding, will keep your hearts and minds safe in union with Jesus Christ.                                    —Philippians 4:7 (TEV)

Last Thanksgiving my mother-in-law came to be with us for the holiday. Since March she had been dealing with cancer, and during her visit she came down with pneumonia. For the next four and one-half months she remained with us, until her death on Maundy Thursday.

Her hospital bed was in the dining room, and she became the nucleus of our family. We all ate together, talked, watched TV, and entertained family and friends together each week. Her inner peace, patience, strength, and courage were glorious to behold. One day I asked her how she was able to cope so well and she told me that she thanked God each day for all her many blessings. How fortunate we were to have her with us.

The joy and inner peace that my mother-in-law had were passed on to all who came in contact with her. The strength that God gave to me, my husband, and our four teenage children was beyond words. It was a beautiful time filled with Christian love, caring, and faith. It was a precious family experience that we will all cherish as long as we live.

*PRAYER:* Dear Lord, thank you for helping us cope with life. Thank you for your great love that is always with us to comfort and sustain us. Amen.

THOUGHT FOR THE DAY

God's peace can be visible in us even in difficult times.

—Lillian Gripp (New Jersey)
*The Upper Room*

# A Fierce and Realistic Peace

There may be no experience in the world that we want more and have less than the experience of peace. The word is everywhere, describing something that is desired but missing— between nations, between people, between the good earth and its inhabitants. Chiefly we tend to notice the absence of peace between our own ears or our own ribs, the absence of tranquility in our own hearts and minds. However much we hanker for peace, we have for the most part learned to live without it. The best most of us can do is to steer our ways through the perilous waters of division and dissent without hitting too many of their floating mines. But the avoidance of conflict is not the same thing as the presence of peace, and that is a truth we carry down in our bones.

Because we know so little about peace, it is hard to say what is missing: a sense of well-being, an inner repose, an abiding calm? I am something of an expert in the pursuit of such virtues, a veteran of diverse efforts to achieve them. I have meditated twenty minutes a day, run twenty miles a week, done good deeds, prayed good prayers; I have reaped the benefits of psychotherapy and massage therapy and a few other therapies in between, but throughout it all what I have not done is gain any lasting hold on peace. I have found ways to rest and refresh myself, for which I am grateful, but meanwhile the world continues to crank out its quota of strife, flattening my hard-won serenity in its path. Whatever I have accomplished with my various disciplines is a personal blessing, but not one that tempers the morning headlines or redeems the evening news.

The ways we have learned to speak about peace do not help me in my dilemma. Consensus suggests that peace consists of harmony in personal relationships and freedom from disquieting thoughts or emotions. Never mind for a moment the impossibility that such conditions can be met for more than five minutes at a time; a peaceful person, by this definition, is one who is untroubled and quietly behaved, which explains how peace and passivity have become synonymous in our time. To hold one's peace means to be quiet, to keep the peace means to obey, to make peace means to surrender, and to rest in peace means, after all, to die. Given these choices, is it any wonder that we feel some ambivalence about whether we want this kind of peace in our lives?

Clearly, a Christian understanding of peace means more than placidity on a personal level or polite resignation on a cultural level. Such simple-minded notions may even be what the founder of our faith renounced when he said that he did not come to bring peace but a sword. His own understanding of peace was a fierce and realistic one: that peace is nothing less than the sure sign of God's presence among us, the be-all and end-all of God's purpose for us, but that it tends to come with sharp edges, with hard choices—that peace tends to come nailed, like himself, to a cross.

For the ancient Hebrews who schooled our Lord the word was shalom, a word so rich that it embraced all the realms of human life. For the individual, shalom meant wholeness, integrity, and self-possession as evidenced by bodily health, longevity, and prosperity. To have shalom meant to enjoy the free, uninhibited growth of the soul in community with others and in right relationship with God.

For the nation of Israel shalom meant peaceful enjoyment of creation and serene communion with God—paradise, in a word, although the Israelites knew little of paradise on earth. It was almost as if they defined peace by what they knew for certain it was not. Survivors of adversity, extermination, and almost eternal homelessness, they used the word to mean loyalty in their relationships, security in their communities, justice in their courts, luck in their commerce, and above all joy in their lives, the sure evidence of God's presence with and favor upon them.

But one thing peace did not mean for the people of Israel was the absence of war, at least not in their lifetime. There were too many predators greedy for their little parcels of land, too many idolators threatening their faith in one God. The chosen people had to fight to live, and so the word peace took on a new meaning for them—peace as the harmony that existed among those who had united for battle. Whether they won or lost, God's blessing seemed evidence to them in their solidarity with one another and with what they believed to be God's purpose for them.

After several hundred years of fighting and mostly losing, however, they began to wonder if they were not doing something wrong. Perhaps they were not obedient enough, not good enough in God's eyes to be defended in battle and rendered victorious over their enemies. Thus peace acquired yet another layer of meaning; it became linked with righteousness, the reward for keeping God's holy laws, upon which divine favor seemed to depend.

One thing was for certain: God alone delivered peace. The Book of Jeremiah is full of that prophet's struggle against the so-called "prophets of well-being," who competed with him by crying, "Peace, peace," when there was no peace. "They prophesy in my name and say that neither sword nor famine shall touch this land," God says to Jeremiah, "but by sword and famine shall those prophets meet their end" (Jer. 14:15, *author paraphrase*).

God is revealed in such passages as something less than a pacifist, as a Lord whose idea of peace had far more to do with the presence of justice than with the absence of struggle. God's peace was not passivity nor peace on the surface nor cheap peace of mind but a deep peace—reached perhaps by equally deep turmoil—and finally recognizable to God alone, so that those who believed learned to ask, "Is it peace?" before they assumed that God's blessing rested on them (cf. 2 Kings 9:17, 18, 22).

Just the same, it was a covenant of peace God wanted above all to establish with Israel, a covenant described in great and gorgeous detail to the prophet Ezekiel. "I will rid the land of wild beasts," the Lord says to him, "and all shall live in peace of mind on the open pastures and sleep in the woods. I will settle them in the neighborhood of my hill and send them rain in due season, blessed rain. Trees in the countryside shall bear their fruit, the land shall yield its produce, and all shall live in peace of mind on their own soil" (Ezekiel 34:25–27, *author paraphrase*)

131

Again and again God let the Israelites know that this covenant would succeed, not because their occasional righteousness had earned them favor but because God had chosen them. Isaiah was the messenger God sent to give Israel the best clues about how God would bridge the gap, how one of no particular beauty or grace would consent to suffer on their account, to endure their torments in order to secure their peace.

That, in brief, is the backdrop against which the Galilean appeared, healing lepers and overturning tables, raising the dead and withering fig trees, altogether speaking out of both sides of his mouth. "You must not think that I have come to bring peace to the earth," he says in the Gospel according to Matthew, but according to John it is his last will and testament. "Peace is my parting gift to you," he said in that account, "my own peace, such as the world cannot give."

Like the ancient Hebrews, our experience of that peace may begin with the recognition of what it is not: not the restlessness that drains our days, or the fear that keeps us up nights, or the rivalry that drives us against and then away from one another. Those are all real parts of our lives in the world, but when we are freed from them—however briefly— by the peace the world cannot give, then we know a different kind of reality. Never mind that it seems always just beyond our grasp, that we cannot attain it once and for all; its purpose may be to keep us on the move, and one moment of true peace is all the seed we need for our lives to bear fruit.

But what does that mean for us day by day? Clearly, it means no one thing. The quest for peace in downtown Beirut will require different strategies than the quest for peace in downtown Detroit, but the vision is the same, a vision that is focused in one who was known four hundred years before his birth as the Prince of Peace, whose life shows us the way of peace, whose death shows us the cost of that way, and whose rising to life again shows us the fullness of his glory. "He *is* our peace," Paul writes in his letter to the Ephesians, and there are ways we are invited to experience that.

If we are disciples of his life, we will above all be reconcilers, seeking always to bring together those who are estranged, whether they are two children in the kitchen, two co-workers at the office, or two world leaders on the scaffolding of war. We will not rest easy with the achievement of mere truce, which is no more than the cessation of hostilities. We may argue, wheedle, cajole, or slam doors, but we will not give up on the truth-telling—about ourselves and others—that precedes all lasting peace.

We will also live in community with others, fellow peacemakers and quarrelers alike, so that peace comes to mean more than personal contentment. We will "enlarge the limits of our homes," in the words of Isaiah, "spread wide the curtains of our tents," learning to work for the good not only of our friends and families but for the good of perfect strangers as well because they are God's kin. We will strengthen not only our wish but our will to forgive those who cross or ignore or use us, as much because it is good for us as because it is good for them.

Finally, we will pray for peace, recognizing where our own power ends and the power of God begins. We will pray with the confidence of those who are doing what they can but who do not delude themselves about the sufficiency of their own efforts. We will remember the one with whom we are in covenant and rely on God to fulfill our purposes since it was God, after all, who put them into our hearts. If we are disciples of Christ's life in these ways, then we will be disciples of his death as well, because the cost of living like that is clear.

Why pray for a peace that costs so much and offers so little immediate comfort? That is a question each believer must wrestle on his or her own. But one possible answer is because it is the only show in town, because if we are disciples of Christ's life and death, than we have glimpsed what it means to be disciples of his risen life as well. And that is the very essence of peace, the least experience of which is enough to draw us on our whole lives long.

We were and are and shall be created in the image of God, whose will for us was and is and shall be peace, a peace that may pass all our understanding but one that is ours nonetheless. The peace of God is real but fleeting, a gift we already possess but one that we have not fully realized. To claim it we may have to surrender our notions of what it is, for peace is offered us not in the absence of struggle but in the presence of almighty God—a peace that comes with a sword, a peace such as the world cannot give, but a peace that promises even now to banish our fears and set our troubled hearts at rest. In that way God's peace is very much a part of God's kingdom. It is a land that is as near to us as it is far off, a land in which we are both citizens and sojourners. While we would like to live in it now, the best we may be able to do for the time being is to live *into* it, rowing a little closer with each choice we make and believing that when we arrive at last it will be by God's grace and in God's own good time.

—Barbara Brown Taylor
*Weavings*

# A Litany for the Family

*Light the first purple candle. Read Isaiah 2:1–4.*

**Leader:** "He will teach us what he wants us to do." That's what the prophet Isaiah said God would do. That's why God sent Jesus to show us what to do.
**All:** What does God want us to do?
**Leader:** God wants us to love each other and be at peace.

**Family Activity:** Talk about ways you can love each other and be at peace in your family. Set up your nativity scene. Put the wise men far away in another part of the room. Remember, they have a long way to travel.

**Prayer:** Dear God, you sent your son to show us how to live. Please help us to understand. Amen.

## Second Sunday in Advent

*Light the first and second purple candles. Read Matthew 3:1–3; Isaiah 11:2–9.*

**Leader:** We should all live together in peace—
**All:** Wolves and sheep.
Leopards and goats,
Calves and lions,
Cows and bears.
**Leader:** They will all live in peace.
**All:** Then why can't we live in peace?

**Family Activity:** Draw a picture of or write down one thing that can make your family more peaceful. Then draw a picture or write down one thing that can make our world more peaceful. Share your drawings and writings with each other. Move the wise men a little closer to the manger.

**Prayer:** God, you know what we wrote down and drew. Please take these as our offering. We want to find ways to bring peace to our families and to our world. Amen.

## Third Sunday in Advent

*Light the first two purple candles and either the pink candle or the third purple candle, whichever your Advent set has. Read Luke 1:46–55.*

Leader: This is the song of praise Mary sang when she learned she would be the mother of God's son. It must have been hard for her, because she was very young, and she wasn't even married yet.

All: People might have called her bad names. They might have laughed at her—and even at Joseph. But that's because they didn't know that Mary's child would be the Messiah.

Leader: But Mary knew. And even though it might have been hard, she was willing to be God's servant.

Family Activity: Think of times when it has been hard for you to do what you knew God wanted you to do. As a family, write a short prayer that you can remember and use during those hard times.

Move the wise men a little closer to the manger.

Prayer: Pray the prayer you wrote together as a family.

## Fourth Sunday in Advent

*Light the first three candles and the final purple candle. Read Isaish 9:2–3, 6.*

Leader: Good news! Isaiah brings us good news!

All: What is the good news?

Leader: God has sent someone to help us, someone who can show us how to love and live in peace.

All: Where is he?

Leader: He has been with us all this time, but we seem to forget until Christmas comes to remind us.

Family Activity: On a calendar for the new year mark a time each month when your family can come together and talk about how God has helped you and about what God wants you to do as a family. Move the wise men a little closer to the manger.

**Prayer:** Dear God, we have heard your good news, and we want to share it with everyone—no more hunger, no more war, no more people hurting people. Help us to be good examples of your good news. Amen.

## Christmas Day

*Light the purple and pink candles in your wreath. Read Luke 2:1–20. Now light the center candle—the white Christ candle—in your wreath.*

**Leader:** This is the day on which the Lord has acted; let us exult and rejoice in it (Psalm 118:24).
**All:** What has God done on this day?
**Leader:** God has sent Jesus to show us God's will for the world.
**All:** What is God's will for the world?
**Leader:** God wants us to
—love each other as brothers and sisters
—care for the world God created
—help those who need it
—trust each other and stop fighting
**All:** Hallelujah and Amen!

**Family Activity:** On a long sheet of paper write in big letters
Hallelujah!
Now decorate your letters any way you want—polka dots, stripes, and happy faces, for example. Hang your Hallelujah! up for all to see.

**Prayer:** Dear God, through your son, Jesus, we are learning how to walk in your way. Please be with us as we try to do your will. And, by the way, God, hallelujah and thank you! Amen.

Move your wise men a little closer to the stable. Each day after Christmas move your wise men a little closer so that on Epiphany (Jan. 6) they will reach the baby Jesus.

# Epiphany

*Read Matthew 2:1–12 Before you begin, bring your wise men to the manger.*

Leader: The journey has been long and hard, but these wise men from the East have finally made their way to the manger.

All: They saw a great light in the sky and followed it.

Leader: They were sky-gazers and star-followers.

All: And their journey brought them to the light of the world, Jesus.

Leader: Their journey tells us that Jesus came for all the world, not just for the Jews.

All: And now it is time for us to begin our journey. It is time for us to be sky-gazers and star-followers.

Leader: Isaiah said, "Arise, shine, for your light has come" (Isaiah 60:1).

Family Activity: Let each member of your family write or draw their answer to this question: What do you think Jesus' coming should mean for the world? Let them write or draw their answers, then silently take their answers and lay them beside the manger as a gift.

Leader: Dear God, like the wise men, we have to dare to take a journey. We must spread the light of the Christmas star over all the world. Be with us as we try to become sky-gazers and star-followers, for the road we travel may not be an easy one.

All: Yes, be with us, God, as we journey in our homes, classrooms, work places, playgrounds, churches, shopping centers—wherever we might be. Amen.

—*Pockets* (staff)

# *Five*

# Epiphany and Beyond

*[The Lord] will teach us
what he wants us to do;
we will walk in the path
he has chosen.*

Isaiah 2:3, TEV

*If you have love for one another,
then everyone will know
that you are my disciples.*

John 13:35, TEV

# The Work of Christmas

When the song of the angels is stilled,
When the star in the sky is gone,
When the kings and princes are home,
When the shepherds are back with their flock,
The work of Christmas begins:
    To find the lost,
    To heal the broken,
    To feed the hungry,
    To release the prisoner,
    To rebuild the nations,
    To bring peace among brothers,
    To make music in the heart.

—**Howard Thurman**
*alive now!*

# For All People

Read Matthew 2:1–12

Now when Jesus was born in Bethlehem of Judea in the days of Herod the King, behold, wise men from the East came to Jerusalem. —Matthew 2:1 (RSV)

When you read the account of the first Christmas, does it seem strange that among the first to worship the Christ Child were foreigners? The Magi had made a long and hazardous journey following a brilliant star, sure that this star would lead them to the child born to be a king.

The shepherds came first to worship the Christ Child. They were poor and illiterate, with no political or religious status. They came in response to a direct message from God. They saw the baby, then hurried away to tell everyone what God had revealed to them.

God's ways are strange to our worldly eyes. A star rises to guide wealthy foreigners to Bethlehem. An angel host appears to lowly shepherds. Could there be a greater difference in the backgrounds of the people who were called by God?

To us these extremes seem strange, but the message of the angel makes it plain. The news of great joy is for *all* people. That means foreigners and natives, wealthy and poor, lowly and mighty. It means even you and me. God's special invitation is for all.

*PRAYER:* Dear God, we accept your invitation to worship you and to carry your message to the world. Amen.

THOUGHT FOR THE DAY

The angel's message of great joy is for everyone.

—Dorothy Enke (Nebraska)
*The Upper Room*

# A Light unto the Gentiles

The Epiphany always comes with snow for us and the steely cold of serious winter, but last year only the cold came. It was a Tuesday, the children already back in school, Sam's patients already back to needing hospital care as well as routine checks, the manuscript load on my desk already stacking up again beyond what I could reach around without a schedule and a duty calendar. I hung one for January on the cork board above my desk and sighed. It was miserably full with no breaks until the kids' first holiday on Martin Luther King's birthday. Christmas was over all right!

The little office off the kitchen where I work was an afterthought in the mind of some previous owner and is attached only on one side to the house. The other three sides jut out like an afterthought should and are walls of windows. I like the openness, the light, the sense of being outside while I work. I can look up from my desk and see our neighbor's barn and garden. I can look south to the pond and Mary's Hill. Behind my desk the windows open east toward our barn and orchard and toward the close and cemetery beyond.

It is a comfortable vista and a comfortable room except when it's extremely cold. Then the wind finds a thousand holes around the storm glasses and the window caulking, under the door, beneath the foundation. The best index to how cold it is is not Sam's outdoor thermometer; it's the inside lower edge of my office door. If there's frost inside the door, it's cold.

Last Epiphany it was cold. The frost on my side of the door had become a layer of ice by the time I sat down to work at eight-thirty. The wind was hungry as a wild dog across the fields. I was amazed, looking toward the close, to see Buckwheat standing in the open field rather than with the herd down by the sheltering trees. Heavy with calf, she was gargantuan in the hard light of the January cold. Her back was covered with frost, her hide sparkling as each blast of wind raised the crystalline jewels on her back and held them to the light. She stood in plain view just beyond the wide gate which allows the pickup to pass from the yard and the orchard to the pastures and the barn. She could not have chosen a more vulnerable spot on so bitter a day and I found myself drawn time and again from the papers before me back to the windows behind me. There was something about her absolute stillness that was almost bothersome. At one point she lay down for a few minutes, but almost immediately she was back up and standing again stock still in the same position she had held for over an hour.

Buckwheat is easily the children's favorite cow and Sam's pet. She's also the biggest cow I have ever seen. Like Saint, she is horned and her span is a good two-and-a-half feet across. Unlike Saint however, she's a good-hearted beast, big enough to be gentle and generous at no expense to herself. But Buckwheat has never liked me. Certainly she's never shown hostility or threatened my right to move freely among the herd. She just doesn't like me.

Animals, like people, have their preferences, their instincts and reactions, and I would never cross them deliberately. So Buckwheat and I have developed an understanding, a kind of ladies' agreement, over the years. When I come into the pasture, she backs away and waits until I am gone. By contrast, the bull is my creature, my pet. So Bull comes to be patted and scratched and Buckwheat leaves, just like a party in the city. Simple rules; simple courtesy.

But Buckwheat, like me or not, is rarely inscrutable and almost never peculiar. Standing there on that open rise in the driving cold was peculiar. I gave it up and settled back down most unwillingly to the galleys in front of me.

In a minute I heard Buckwheat do something. It was hardly a moo, and only bulls bellow, but the sound was somewhere closer to bellow than moo. Had she been a goose, I would have said she honked, if you can imagine a one-ton honk.

In a minute the sound came again. I turned around and looked toward the gate. Just as I looked, Buckwheat lowered her head six inches, extended her neck and let out a honk to

144

end all honks. Then she turned her head, looked straight at the office windows and waited. I stood up and went over to the window through which she could undoubtedly see my movement if not me. She honked again, this time looking right at the house and sending that distressing noise over me. Then she lowered her head to the ground and began to bob it as she licked and nuzzled the black mound of stuff on the ground in front of her.

She had calved! That dumb cow had chosen the coldest, windiest spot on the whole frozen farm to calve in! Sam had just checked her last night and she had shown no signs of being ready. Now she had done this stupid thing. I was annoyed beyond speech...until it dawned on me that Buckwheat is not a dumb cow. Nor is she original. She is, as a matter of fact, bright as cows go, the leader of the herd when Bull is elsewhere. But it goes against all the instincts and habits of cows to do their birthing in the open and/or especially around people, so why as near the house as she could get on top of the most exposed rise she could find?

She honked again and licked some more. The calf raised its head and lowered it. I was sorely tempted to bundle up and at least step out as far as the gate to see the size of the little fellow, but knowing Buckwheat, I knew she wouldn't like my coming that near.

She honked again. Darned cow! What in the world was wrong with her? I'd never heard such a sound in all my years with cows. In irritation I went back to my desk and passed a boring ten minutes chasing errors, mostly commas. *Why all typesetters are in love with commas beats me,* I thought as I deleted the fourth superfluous one in as many pages. Buckwheat honked. I stood up and looked out. The calf was still lying on the ground and the afterbirth had come. As I leaned toward the window to see better, Buckwheat bellowed again as if she had found a whole new line of conversation and intended to stick with it for the rest of our days together.

The phone rang and I talked, endlessly it seemed, although I can't remember now to whom or about what. It was ten-thirty already, I realized, and went to make myself some tea to warm my fingers. Buckwheat was still nuzzling and licking. Ten-thirty! That calf should be up by now. Should be nursing. Should be moving. That calf was freezing!

That was why she had come! The barn paddocks were closed because we hadn't thought it was time yet to put her up and she had done the only other possible thing. She had come for help. The most aloof and self-sufficient of the whole lot had come for help.

I watched for what seemed like hours, but by the clock was no more than a quarter of an hour. If I went out, I would have to take the calf in order to save it. Given her consistent distrust of me, she would (or so I surmised) charge me to defend the calf. Even assuming she could be cajoled—a silly assumption right from the start—the minute I picked the calf up it would have my odor even in the cold, and she would forever reject it. A motherless calf in the deep winter has less than no chance to survive, even given all the human help possible.

As if reading the space between us, Buckwheat gave one last bellow, moved away from the calf and lay down. *All right,* I thought, *a fair offer deserves a fair chance.* To leave the calf, still wet from birthing, any longer in the wind would be to lose it. If she were to charge, I would be alone. I would be the one lying in the pasture unable to escape the zero weather.

The calf did not move at all now. I could no longer detect its breathing even. Buckwheat was as silent as she had been loud. It was my decision.

I wrapped Sam's huge duck-down coat around me. I might need its warmth desperately and its thickness might absorb a horn if she only grazed me.

I went as far as the gate. Buckwheat turned her head, looked straight at me for a full minute, and then turned away. The calf did not appear to be breathing. I opened the gate, leaving it ajar behind me for hasty retreat, and slipped over into Buckwheat's territory. She did not move. The ice on her back glittered as the sun came out briefly from behind a cloud. The meadow was quiet as death. I moved toward the calf. Nothing happened.

I stooped and put my hand out to touch its side and see if it were still breathing. As I touched, Buckwheat rose regally to her feet. For so large an animal she is graceful and agile beyond belief. She stood not ten feet from me, upright on all four feet, and looked down where I squatted beside her calf. At fifty I was large all right, but no longer agile and never graceful. And I think she thought it over. For just one portion of a second, I think she considered her advantage and then rejected it. She moved to her left upwind of me as if my odor still offended intolerably even in her hour of need. I picked up the inert calf. Safely in my arms, it opened an eye. Frozen, yes, but not yet dead.

I turned my back on Buckwheat and headed out the gate. As I turned to lock it back behind me, I looked straight into Buckwheat's face. She had followed us so stealthily that even the cracking grass had not betrayed her. I realized instantly that she could once more have had me had she wished. She hadn't wished. I locked the gate and carried the calf into the house.

Like every farmhouse ours has its sizeable supply of old blankets, spreads, sheets and rags. I gathered up two or three and wiped the motionless calf dry and then wrapped the whole thing in more blankets. Nothing happened—no sound, no movement, no twitch. I turned on the space heater and almost as quickly took off Sam's coat. It was ninety degrees in that kitchen. Still no response from the calf.

Finally, I did the only thing I knew to do. I sat down on the floor crosslegged and took Buckwheat's calf into the warmth of my body, circling it as best I could with my arms and my legs. At least I could feel it still breathing that way.

And I sat there just waiting, for what I don't know. My mind began to wander as minds do, of course. Suddenly I came back from my daydreaming and realized that I was rocking the calf and singing to it as I had sung to so many other Tickles before it. And the calf had opened her eyes. By lunch, as we sat on the floor together, she had begun to wiggle. Shortly thereafter she tried to nurse my sleeve and I knew we were home free.

I set the calf down and tried to wake up all the parts of my body that had long since even ceased to hurt. Buckwheat, when I looked out, was still standing at the gate.

The calf behind me tried to stand up and fell smack down on the slick kitchen floor. But it protested. It protested rather firmly in fact. I carried her into the carpeted office and she stood up immediately. Over the next hour she investigated the whole office, sucked on every projection, and bawled twice. She even, while I was making myself a sandwich, wobbled across the kitchen floor, negotiating it successfully this time, and made it to the living room.

A calf in the living room is like a plow on the front porch, too much even for me. I picked Covenant up. I had done the naming this time. The galleys she had interrupted by her precipitous arrival were a novel called *Covenant at Coldwater* by John Osier. The name had come to me sometime during my crooning, I suppose. I wasn't even conscious of any decision, but Covenant it was and still is.

So I picked Covenant up and out we went to the orchard. Whether she was going to be Buckwheat's now or ours to try to nourish on a bottle, we had to know. Not only was the living room too much, but she was weakening from hunger. Covenant shone dry and jet back in my arms as I carried her to the pear trees and set her down. Buckwheat watched. I went to the gate. Buckwheat stepped back as was her custom. I swung the gate wide. Still she hesitated. I moved back into the garden and she came through the untended gate into the orchard. I locked the gate behind her and left as quickly as possible.

Back into the house I went and out the front door to the back far corner of the yard from where I could watch the orchard undetected. Covenant was already nursing by the time I got there. Good! I would leave them until Sam got home. They would follow him to the barn with no prodding. The adventure, if not the day, was over, and the galleys were still waiting on my desk.

I put the rags in to wash and cleaned up the kitchen. The children would be home soon. Too late to really begin anything on my desk now. I sat down in my big desk chair and dozed for a minute.

I'd never thought much about Epiphany, never had any significant event to mark it before. The giving of the Child to

148

the Gentiles. Certainly there had been nothing godly about my day and there would never be anything divine about Buckwheat. Yet I had never wondered before about Joseph. Why had he let the kings in? Did he need their gifts for his escape, need them to buy his Son safe passage to Egypt? Why would a Jew allow Gentile hands to touch what he must have known by then was sacred? Did need drive Joseph as it had driven Buckwheat? Did it take him to the despised and disgusting, to those whose very odor was an offense? I was fascinated by my dozing reverie.

The bell rang. Kids home and loud from school. No more thoughts until supper when, the calf and her mama safely in the barn and the house quiet around us, I blew out the Christ Candle for the last time till next Christmas. As I did, I said to Sam, "Thank goodness we never have everything we need without having to ask each other."

"Thinking about Buckwheat and Covie?" he asked smiling.

"Yeah," I said. "I never rocked a calf before," but really I was thinking of Joseph and how the light came to the Gentiles.

—Phyllis A. Tickle
*What the Heart Already Knows*

# The Matter-of-Fact Guard

Read Mark 6:14–29

The guard left, went to the prison, and cut John's head off.
—Mark 6:27 (TEV)

What about the guard in the story of John the Baptist's death? Such cool dispatch, so matter-of-fact. None of this agonizing, moral-dilemma stuff for him. He snapped to and obeyed Herod's order "at once." A model of discipline. Single-minded. Did he speak to John before beheading him? Did John speak to him?

When I see poor people standing in a soup line or read that mostly the elderly, women, and children have to bear 40 percent of the domestic budget cutbacks, do I merely stifle a yawn? When I am told by exiled South Africans that it is their government's plan to relocate 1,000 "economic units" (black Africans) per day for the next 20 years to barren "homelands" (wastelands) denying them citizenship and dooming them to economic decay, do I merely say, "How interesting"?

Did the guard who followed orders subsequently have trouble sleeping nights? Thank God I am not like that guard. Or am I?

PRAYER: Dear God, forgive me when I choose to be blind to injustice and human cruelty. Give me courage to question wrongdoing and to overcome evil with good. Amen.

THOUGHT FOR THE DAY

To ignore the suffering of others makes us less human.

—Marcia W. Graham (Indiana)
*The Upper Room*

# God Who Intervenes

Read Exodus 37:7–12

The Lord said, "I have seen the affliction of my people."
—Exodus 3:7 (RSV)

I was watching a swimming class in progress. A few students were trying painstakingly to swim according to instructions from the coach, who was closely watching each one of his trainees in the pool. Suddenly I heard a splash, and I saw the coach swimming across, carrying one of his trainees who could swim no longer because of fatigue.

I then remembered what took place at Mount Horeb, when God spoke to Moses, "I have seen the affliction of my people . . . and have heard their cry because of their taskmasters; I know their sufferings, and I have come down to deliver them."

God is closely watching us in all our struggles and comes to us in the midst of our agony and suffering. God is no onlooker; God intervenes in history through people to deliver us from our bondages and alienations. It is God's leap into history that we see in Bethlehem's manger. And the message of God's kingdom which Jesus announced—good news to the poor—invites us to participate in the struggles of people to help release them from bondage.

PRAYER: O God, we thank you for your eternal vigil for us. Help us to break free from all fetters of bondage by relying on you. Make us instruments to free others. Amen.

THOUGHT FOR THE DAY

God frees us to free others.

—Joseph Ayrookuzhy (Kerala, India)
*The Upper Room*

# A Living Sign

I know not always how God comes,
    but that God comes—this I know:
        in an obscure stable,
        in splashing waters,
        in the breaking of bread
and often, my friend,
incarnate in you,
for God, I believe, still comes in the flesh, in
people.

Now and always
    may the Christ in you
    keep you
        a sign of living love
        and love living among us.

—Bonnie B. Belasic
*alive now!*

152

# Christ Lives among Us

Within a few days it will be Christmas. Toward the end of December, we will celebrate the birth of a child: small, meek, tender, vulnerable, appealing. A baby will be in our midst. It will not threaten nor carry any power. It will require only those things necessary for personal survival and growth.

Lying in his cradle, Jesus will not request us to be poor in spirit. He will not bring any religious leaders to task. He will not mingle with the rejects of society. He will not call us phonies nor whited sepulchers. He will not upset our money tables. We can be quite tender with baby Jesus.

When he enters adulthood, we begin having mixed feelings about him. He turns the tables on us, and his adult demands are disconcerting. They shake our value systems. They force us to reflect upon our behavior and to examine our commitments.

As an adult he cannot be cuddled nor cooed over. He presents a facet of himself we had not expected. He becomes perceptive, incisive, demanding our best. He speaks with authority, inviting us to make him the center of our lives. That makes us uncomfortable.

He upsets routine. He breaks up families. He sleeps in foxholes. He lies naked on a cross. He expects us to follow him.

What a contrast the adult Jesus is to the powerless baby lying on the straw. Both tug at the heartstrings of humanity. Yet friendship with the adult is different from friendship with the child. Both solicit love. Yet caressing the baby is not the same as responding to the mature person.

Let us enjoy this memorable birthday which brought into history the God who changed the destiny of humanity. But let us also remember that, eventually, we need to let go of the cuddly baby. We need to permit the powerful Christ to enter our lives, even at the risk of changing them.

—Loretta Girzaitis
*alive now!*

# Putting Away the Bows

Read Philippians 2:1–11

You have fellowship with the Spirit, and you have kindness and compassion for one another.    —Philippians 2:1 (TEV)

The frantic last minute rush is over. Bright, bow-bedecked packages have disappeared from under the tree, and a rainbow of crumpled paper spills out of a large cardboard carton.

Bows and curly ribbons, saved each year, have been carefully placed in a box. As I tape it closed, I begin thinking. These bows were used on presents that were bought and wrapped while our hearts were overflowing with the warm, loving spirit of giving, the Christmas spirit. No gift was too expensive or too hard to find if it would make someone we loved happy.

Now, I wonder, will we pack away that generous spirit along with the bows, to be brought out again next year? Tomorrow, will we forget the joy of today? Will we still be willing to help fill a food basket for a needy family, clothe a naked child, set aside grievances, or forgive a sharp word?

If we shared our lives with the same generosity and warmth as that with which Christmas gifts are given, we would be honoring Christ the entire year.

PRAYER: Lord, help us to nourish the loving spirit we have shared with others this season, so it gives others happiness and serves you throughout the year. Amen.

THOUGHT FOR THE DAY

Hang on to the Christmas spirit.

—June M. Boone (Tennessee)
*The Upper Room*

# Worn, Faded, and Beautiful

Read 2 Corinthians 4:1–12

*Paul wrote,* "We have this treasure in earthen vessels, to show that the transcendent power belongs to God and not to us." —2 Corinthians 4:7 (RSV)

The white pitcher's once-bright finish is now dulled with time. Embellished by tinges of brown, a checkerboard pattern of cracks is scattered across the glaze. On one side there is the faint imprint of a bouquet of pink and blue flowers. The scalloped lip of the pitcher dips at one edge, forming a shallow spout. The handle is gracefully curved, and the body widens as it nears the base. The charm of the pitcher lies in the character etched by the years into its finish. The faded bouquet imprinted on its side betrays countless washings. The pitcher has grown beautiful not by being set upon a shelf in some china cabinet but by being used over the years. The finish has worn, the flowers have faded, and the pitcher has become beautiful, like a face creased by years of laughing.

Christians, like pitchers, are made for a particular purpose. God bestows gifts on each of us that we may enrich the lives of others. With years of service, we become beautiful—not because we have been saved high on a shelf where we cannot be marred but because we have been used for God's purposes.

*PRAYER:* Dear God, help us open ourselves to being used again and again for your work. Amen.

THOUGHT FOR THE DAY

We become beautiful as we allow ourselves to be used for God's purposes.

—Stephanie Whitson (Nebraska)
*The Upper Room*

# How Do We Return?

Read Luke 2:15–20

Whatever you do, in word or deed, do everything in the name of the Lord Jesus, giving thanks to God the Father through him. —Colossians 3:17 (RSV)

The shepherds were privileged to be a part of that first Christmas. They heard the angelic message proclaiming the birth of the Messiah and were evidently among the first to worship in Jesus' presence. What joy must have filled their hearts! How excited they must have been! Eventually, however, they had to return to the fields. The coming of the Messiah did not negate the need for shepherds to care for the flocks. But the important thing is how they returned. They did not go back in sadness and dejection because the great event was over and now they had to return to the routine of their daily work. Instead, they "returned, glorifying and praising God."

Once again this year, Christmas is past for us, and we too must return—to our job, our school, our housework. How do we return? Is it with a sense of sadness and dread because we have to encounter the same routine, the same people, the same problems? Or are we able to return with a renewed joy and vigor in our lives for having been reminded once again of God's great love and great gift?

*PRAYER:* Dear God, help us to thank you, praise you, and glorify you in the midst of our daily lives. In the name of Jesus we pray. Amen.

THOUGHT FOR THE DAY

Am I glorifying God by my attitudes?

—Cora Lee Pless (North Carolina)
*The Upper Room*

# The Kings' Return

We must go home.
No simple return trip,
ticking off landmarks,
rewinding the cord
of our travels.
The string's been cut
that measured out our miles.
We're shaken loose by Truth
which throws us back
toward the neglected,
too familiar place
where incarnation's to be lived.
Emboldened by encounter
we set forth
toward the unknown,
toward home.

—Ellen Roberts Young
*alive now!*

# Song of the Magi

The path away
   is every bit as important as
the path which approaches:
   maybe more.

For we were led to God's son,
   gave him our gifts,
   and were changed forever.

Thus we leave
   lighter
   yet bearing a different, welcome burden.

What path now to follow?
And where is home?

—James C. Huffstutler
*alive now!*

# Author Index